Thinking About Sex

Thinking About Sex

Adrian Thatcher

Fortress Press

Minneapolis

THINKING ABOUT SEX

Fortress Press Edition © 2015
Copyright © Adrian Thatcher 2012

This book is published in cooperation with Society for Promoting Christian Knowledge, London, England. Originally titled *Making Sense of Sex*. Interior contents have not been changed.

All rights reserved. Except for brief quotations in critical articles or reviews, no part of this book may be reproduced in any manner without prior written permission from the publisher. Visit http://www.augsburgfortress.org/copyrights/contact.asp or write to Permissions, Augsburg Fortress, Box 1209, Minneapolis, MN 55440.

Unless otherwise noted, Scripture quotations are taken or adapted from the HOLY BIBLE, NEW INTERNATIONAL VERSION. Copyright © 1973, 1978, 1984 by International Bible Society.

Quotations marked KJV are from the Authorized Version of the Bible (The King James Bible), the rights in which are vested in the Crown, and are reproduced by permission of the Crown's Patentee, Cambridge University Press.

Quotations marked REB are from the Revised English Bible, copyright © Oxford University Press and Cambridge University Press 1989.

Library of Congress Cataloging-in-Publication Data
Print ISBN: 978-1-5064-0069-3
eBook ISBN: 978-1-5064-0099-0

The paper used in this publication meets the minimum requirements of American National Standard for Information Services—Permanence of Paper for Printed Library Materials, ANSIZ329.48-1984.

Manufactured in the U.S.A.

In felicem memoriam
Grace Thatcher, 1943–2002
post suam mortem decem annos
requiescat in vita aeterna
('In happy memory, ten years after her death;
may she rest in eternal life')

Contents

1. Making sense of the sources — 1
2. Making sense of desire – from repression to expression — 16
3. Making sense of bodies – from 'sinful bodies' to the Body of Christ — 29
4. Making sense of sexual difference – from difference to indifference — 42
5. Making sense of homosexuality – from disgust to delight — 56
6. Making sense of marriage – from patriarchy to partnership — 69
7. Making sense of Spirit – from crucifixion to inspiration — 85

Notes — 90

Further reading — 102

1

Making sense of the sources

In this first chapter the question *how* Christians might make sense of sex is discussed. First, several barriers to understanding are named and removed. Second, the sources that are available for Christians to use for making sense of sex are described. Third, the approach of Liberal Theology to making sense of sex is outlined.

Making sense of *sex*?

Making sense of sex is a very tall order indeed. This volume belongs to a series of 'Making Sense of' books. God's love, the Bible, and so on, are subjects we can try and make some sense of. But when it comes to sex, *we* are the subjects. We are *sexed*: we have a sex. Many of us *have* sex. The puzzle is of a different order because we ourselves are part of the puzzle.

All living creatures are sexed. They need to be roughly male or female in order to reproduce. But human beings are reflective, self-conscious creatures. When we want to have sex, we know we do. Human beings belong to societies where traditions about who can have sex with whom, and how, and when, are centuries old. Powerful instincts are hedged about with regulation and constraint. But these constraints, and our acceptance of them, are not, like God, everlasting. Conventions change, yet still our innermost desires often conflict with them.

Making sense of sex assumes that there is some possible way of understanding it, and so of arriving at a *rational* grasp of some of our basic instincts and drives. Even this assumption is problematic. Not only can the power of desire overwhelm our moral convictions, the argument over which is the stronger – reason or passion – is an old and inconclusive one. Sex seems to elude codification and control.

Having sex cannot be separated out from wider issues of gender, and so of power and dominance, powerlessness and surrender, vulnerability as well as ecstasy, and often fear, comedy and tragedy. Rowan Williams summed up the multiple ambiguities of sex by asking:

> Why does sex matter? Most people know that sexual intimacy is in some ways frightening for them, that it is quite simply the place where they began to be taught whatever maturity they have. Most of us know that the whole business is irredeemably comic, surrounded by so many odd chances and so many opportunities for making a fool of yourself. Plenty know that it is the place where they are liable to be most profoundly damaged or helpless. Culture in general and religion in particular have devoted enormous energy to the doomed task of getting it right.[1]

Is getting sex right doomed from the start? Williams is clear that we are never going to get sex right. But the inevitable failure to get it right does not amount to a sexual pessimism about sexual encounters or relationships. It is the beginning of a proper and theological understanding of sex. He continues: 'I want to try and understand a little better why the task is doomed, and why the fact that it's doomed is a key to seeing more fully why and how it matters – and even seeing more fully what this mattering has to do with God.'

Not getting sex right, on this view, is the key to making sense of it. Through our failings and fumblings we may become wiser.

Barriers to understanding

Very many people, including not a few Christians, do not find the Christian tradition very helpful for making sense of sex. It is not that people wilfully forsake a demanding sexual ethic for a more easy-going worldly one. It is that they often cannot see the point of its 'demandingness'. The Roman Catholic Church has the strictest teachings of all denominations. Plenty of Christians, including Catholics, cannot see the point of remaining within a marriage that is spiritually dead, or forbidding the use of condoms to millions of people in the grip of the HIV & AIDS pandemic. Plenty of lesbian and gay Christians cannot see the point of the teachings raised against them. Plenty of Christians cannot see the point of refraining from sex until marriage (usually in their late twenties, or early thirties) or from masturbating if they feel like it.

Christians try to *obey* God. The problem, of course, is that the will of God must first be known before it can be obeyed. The Christian faith is changing, and the Christian understanding of the character of God is changing too. Many Christians just can't make sense of a God who requires constant heroic resistance to the very desires that God has placed in us. It is not that the counter-cultural demand of Christian witness is being refused. Radical obedience requires radical reasons for it to be sustained. Traditional teachings about sex and gender are one of the reasons why people left the Church in the 1960s.[2]

Dualism

There are at least three other reasons why the Christian tradition, especially in its conservative forms, may be thought to be unhelpful in making sense of sex. These can be labelled *dualism*, *sexism* and *pessimism*. Dualism is any view that assumes that one thing is really two things (*duo* in Latin). A standard Christian view, held by a clear majority of theologians, is set out in the Roman Catholic *Catechism*:

> The unity of soul and body is so profound that one has to consider the soul to be the 'form' of the body: i.e., it is because of its spiritual soul that the body matter becomes a living, human body; spirit and matter, in man, are not two natures united, but rather their union forms a single nature.[3]

This view (standard since St Thomas Aquinas in the thirteenth century) is obviously not dualistic, for it combines soul and body, and spirit and matter within a 'unity'. It has the name *holism* (from the Greek, *holos*, 'whole'). The problem is that much Christian thought is holistic in theory, yet thoroughly dualistic in practice. It can maintain the unity of the person while allowing a disastrous devaluation of the body in relation to the soul.[4]

Nearly 20 years ago I analysed dualism by means of six pairs of opposites. They were:

Soul	Body
Reason	Passion
Will	Desire
Spirit	Flesh
Culture	Nature
Public	Private[5]

It is easy to see the havoc that these pairs of opposites can cause for human self-understanding. The first four terms on the left have come to represent the spiritual side of the person, that which is eternal, incorporeal and most like God. The first four terms on the right have come to represent the temporal, corporeal side of the human person – mortal, frail and fallen. The terms on the left are *privileged* in relation to their counterparts on the right. All six pairs are often depicted as in conflict with each other, so that the person becomes the site of conflict between opposing forces; between a 'microcosm' (a tiny world) within and a 'macrocosm' (the world further out).

Sexism

It has become clear that soul/body dualism fosters another kind of dualism, *male/female* dualism, or (to use a contemporary term) *sexism*. In the last 20 years *gender*, 'the relations between women and men',[6] has been intensively studied and the Christian tradition has been shown to be lacking in its contribution to taking seriously the full personhood of women. Many contemporary Christians, I suspect, have little idea of how women have been regarded in Christian tradition. The attitude of Jesus towards women was very different from that of theologians in the intervening centuries between the Bible and our own times. Until recently men were thought to be closely associated with soul, reason, will and spirit; women with body, passion, desire and flesh. That explains why men were identified with culture, women with nature; men with the public, women with the private world (the fifth and sixth pairs of opposites). It also explains why men got an education, occupied the professions and ran the world.

> Many contemporary Christians have little idea of how women have been regarded in Christian tradition

Making sense of the sources

'Incarnation' or 'excarnation'?

Christianity is distinctive by its belief that God has come and lived among us. John's Gospel says, 'The Word became flesh and made his dwelling among us' (John 1.14). The name given to Christ's coming among us as flesh is *incarnation*. An incarnational faith might be thought to be lived out in the encounters of fleshly bodies. However, another concept, *excarnation*, has recently appeared, and it well captures what has happened to Christianity in the last 500 years. The flesh has been ejected in favour of a faith that is much more, if not completely, cerebral in its reception and expression. Charles Taylor (in a very long and dense book) shows how 'official Christianity has gone through what we can call an "excarnation", a transfer out of embodied, "enfleshed" forms of religious life, to those which are more "in the head"'.[7] In a prophetic passage, he says:

> We tend to live in our heads, trusting our disengaged understandings: of experience, of beauty . . . even the ethical: we think that the only valid form of ethical self-direction is through rational maxims or understanding. We can't accept that part of being good is opening ourselves to certain feelings; either the horror at infanticide, or agape as a gut feeling.[8]

There are, of course, reactions to this longer-term historical process. Late modern promiscuity is a good example of a *return* to incarnation (but hardly a 're-incarnation'!) where living in and through the heightened experience of the body has become the supreme good. A believable Christian faith must own up to its part in bringing about this excarnation, and offer its adherents an alternative to the fleshly indulgences of a decadent capitalist culture. The alternative must make sense both of the God-given pleasures of intimacy and the enormous responsibilities that accompany the sharing of it. This book tries to do this.

Donna Freitas' recent study of sexual experience on college campuses in the USA, *Sex and the Soul*,[9] indicates the necessity of a balanced theology of sex which avoids the extremes of the 'hook-up culture' on the one hand, and the 'no-sex-thank-you-we-are-evangelicals' on the other. Only in evangelical colleges is there serious opposition to the hook-up culture and Freitas rightly commends them for this. However, there is a high price to be paid among the students – in her terms, the drastic sundering of sexual experience from their souls.

Making sense of the sources

Dualism rules once more. The evangelical ethos (among its many other characteristics)

> exacts demands on students that can be severe, debilitating and often unrealistic. The pressures to marry are extreme for women, and college success is often determined by a ring, not a diploma. Because of the strong hold of purity culture, many students learn to practise sexual secrecy, professing chastity in public while keeping their honest feelings and often their actual experiences hidden.[10]

These attitudes are not confined to American campuses; they are common in the Church. Again, this book offers a middle way, drawing on the resources of Liberal Theology in order to promote a mature union of spirituality and sexuality together.

Pessimism

Some Christians are deeply pessimistic about the social trends towards greater sexual freedom. We have just discussed the distressing prevalence of promiscuity. It is possible to see pre-marital sex, rising divorce rates, abortion, promiscuity, the tolerance of homosexuality, the legalization of civil partnerships, and so on, as evidence of late modern decadence. Sexual sins are thought to be evidence of the weakening of religious faith, of growing secularization, and of a falling away from a proud and devout Christian past. In fact the situation is immensely more complicated. There is another way of reading social changes, where the acknowledgement of human rights and the increase in social justice have made steady gains over racism, sexism, patriarchalism and colonialism (all of which derived much succour from Christianity). It is no longer a requirement to remain locked in a destructive marriage. Marital rape is now a crime. There is no longer a need for foundling hospitals to care for abandoned children. Bastardy, that terrible stigma, is dismantled.[11] Reproductive life can be regulated – an absolutely necessary ability if the earth is not to exhaust itself. Love and commitment between same-sex partners is now legally recognized.

Jeffrey Weeks' book *The World We Have Won* actually celebrates the achievements of late modern culture in the sphere of sexual intimacy. Looking back to developments since 1945 the author believes 'the long revolution to have been overwhelmingly beneficial to the vast majority of people in the West, and increasingly to people living in the global South whose lives are also being transformed dramatically'.[12] He calls this 'the democratization of everyday life'. That judgement is at least a possible one to consider, even though serious problems of promiscuity and injustice for children remain. It is not necessary for Christians to be pessimists about sex (or about anything else). They can be grateful realists instead.

Sources for making sense of sex

In the next two sections, theological sources and the character of Liberal Theology are discussed. Readers who want to get straight to the sex and gender issues that occupy the rest of the book, without worrying about prior considerations, can safely skip to Chapter 2 now.

Scripture, Tradition and Reason

It might be helpful to say there are six of these sources. The first three are Scripture, Tradition and Reason.[13] Most Christians agree about these, but disagree about the extent to which each is valued in relation to the others. All Christians agree that the Bible is our primary source for learning about the Faith. They disagree about what the Bible is, and about the authority it has in, and over, the churches. Anglican bishops recommend a twofold reading strategy. When discussing 'the use of the Bible in sexual ethics', they commend reading it

> as a witness to the grace of God through which salvation is offered to us in fulfilment of God's covenant promises, and as guide to the path of Christian discipleship... In terms of the specific issue of human sexuality it means reading the Bible in such a way as to discover how God's will for human sexual conduct gives expression to his grace.[14]

The problem the bishops do not discuss is the obvious incompatibility between reading the Bible as a *witness* to God's actions in Jesus Christ, and reading the Bible as a *guidebook*.[15] The main problem is the confusion between being a *witness* to the Revelation and being the Revelation itself. (Think about being a witness to a crime. Witnessing a crime is utterly different from committing a crime.) This is a sticking point for liberal Christians. They are unlikely to say that the Bible is the Word of God, not because they think that the Bible is unimportant, but because it confuses Jesus, who *is* the Word of God in the flesh, with the *witness* to the Word of God which the Bible is.

> It confuses Jesus, who *is* the Word of God in the flesh, with the *witness* to the Word of God which the Bible is

Once the Bible becomes the guidebook to sexual conduct, looking up passages to see what is forbidden or allowed becomes an irresistible temptation.

The Roman Catholic and Orthodox Churches give equal weight to Scripture and Tradition. The Roman Catholic Church believes that there are 'two distinct modes of transmission' of God's revelation – 'Sacred Tradition and Sacred Scripture'.[16] Scripture 'is the speech of God as it is put down in writing under the breath of the Holy Spirit'. Tradition 'transmits in its entirety the Word of God which has been entrusted to the apostles by Christ the Lord and the Holy Spirit'. Catholics derive 'certainty' from both, and each 'must be accepted and honoured with equal sentiments of devotion and reverence'.

There are several problems with these assertions. Assuming we can identify 'Tradition', some pretty ghastly teachings and practices are inescapably embedded in it. Was the Inquisition, or the burning of heretics, an authentic transmission of God's Word? There needs to be a way of discerning which bits of Tradition authentically transmit the Word of God. Protestants don't generally give Tradition much time. But they neglect it at their peril. It is through Tradition that every generation of Christians has a direct link to the founding events of the faith, and beyond, through the First Testament,[17] into the infancy of the human race. Christians have *made* Tradition, and there is much we can learn from their wisdom, as well as from their mistakes. And Tradition goes on being made. We make it ourselves. The Anglican bishops helpfully remind Christians of the 'need to test tradition against the Scriptures themselves and against the moral convictions of contemporary society, and remember that even the most venerable traditions can be wrong or inappropriate for today'.[18]

> Christians have *made* Tradition, and there is much we can learn from their wisdom, as well as from their mistakes

Making sense of the sources

Anglicans also hold Reason as a source of theology, sometimes seeing it as the third leg of a 'three-legged stool'. Reason is very important for liberal Christians, including at one time most Anglicans, because what we can find out about ourselves and our world by asking questions, developing hypotheses, performing experiments, and so on, also helps us to find about God and God's ways with the world. There are things that God reveals to us because we are otherwise incapable of finding them out; but most things we know we can find out for ourselves. Christians who stress the importance of Reason do not want to abandon the conviction that God is revealed in Scripture and Tradition, and supremely in Christ. They say that there is no obvious contradiction between Reason and Revelation, between human inquiry and divine disclosure, between science and theology. Liberal Christians have an important place for Reason and Tradition because they see many Protestant churches placing an exaggerated emphasis on the Bible, and on a literal reading of it, to the neglect of what God allows us to know by other means.

Experience, Conscience and Wisdom

A fourth source is Experience. There are inconclusive arguments about whether Experience is a separate source or whether it is better included in the category of Reason. I am convinced that Experience should be regarded as a separate source,[19] especially when trying to make sense of sex, for our sexual experiences may be the most character-forming experiences we ever have. Writers who subsume Experience within the category of Reason may be too swayed by the idea that the image of God in

> Our sexual experiences may be the most character-forming experiences we ever have

humankind is better expressed by our rational faculties than by any other. While not denying reason is a gift of God, I don't think reason can be privileged over passion, for God is passionate too.

A fifth source is Conscience. Religious and secular thought alike hold to a faculty which helps us to distinguish between right and wrong actions, and leads to feelings either of rectitude or of remorse. Conscience (in Latin, Greek and English) is literally a 'knowing together with', which rather contradicts the idea that conscience is best understood as an 'inner voice' or moral alarm bell that rings unexpectedly. It is rather the ability to acquire moral knowledge in co-operation with other people, and especially with people who are affected by our actions. Conscience helps us to turn regret into resolve – into an opportunity not to repeat past mistakes and vices.

Finally, Wisdom is a source of theology and ethics. The early Anglican theologian Richard Hooker wrote of God's Wisdom:

> As her ways are of sundry kinds, so her manner of teaching is not merely one and the same. Some things she openeth by the sacred books of Scripture; some things by the glorious works of Nature: with some things she inspireth them from above by spiritual influence; in some things she leadeth and traineth them only by world experience and practice. We may not so in any one special kind admire her, that we disgrace her in any other; but let all her ways be according unto their place and degree adored.[20]

These words of Hooker are themselves wise. Wisdom teaches us; that is what wisdom does (Proverbs 8). The wisdom here is God's but it is imparted to us, and Hooker's account of the way wisdom is imparted is very significant. Wisdom is broader than even Scripture, Tradition and Reason. Wisdom uses Scripture to teach us. But She also uses our knowledge of the 'works of Nature'. Sometimes She influences us directly: at other times She uses our involvement in the secular world ('world experience and practice') to confront us with new but divinely sourced knowledge. Wisdom lies at the root of all the other sources of theological knowledge, and She is honoured when discovered appropriately in each one.

In the end, all six sources present themselves to us as *resources* for enabling us, in common with other Christians, to love God, our neighbours, and ourselves, better than we otherwise would. They give us *doctrine*. Christian sexual ethics should take the core doctrine that 'God is love' (1 John 4.8, 16)[21] much more seriously. Yet that supreme basis of the Christian life is often compromised by lesser appeals to regulation and prohibition. The Great Commandments of Jesus insist that *love* is the first and last requirement of his followers:

> Jesus replied: '"Love the Lord your God with all your heart and with all your soul and with all your mind." This is the first and greatest commandment. And the second is like it: "Love your neighbour as yourself." All the Law and the Prophets hang on these two commandments.'
>
> (Matt. 22.37–40)

The approach of Liberal Theology

The approach to making sense of sex in this book is unashamedly and wholeheartedly *liberal*. The 'Making Sense of' series is self-consciously liberal in its approach to its topics, and the theological society that suggested the series, Modern Church, defines itself as an 'organisation that promotes liberal Christian theology'.[22] What then, is Liberal Theology?

What Liberal Theology is not

We can start by saying what Liberal Theology is not. It is not fundamentalist;[23] it is not conservative evangelical;[24] and it is not Roman Catholic. Fundamentalists think that the Bible is infallible, that every word of it is dictated by God the Holy Spirit to human authors. Fundamentalism is daft but dangerous. It ignores obvious problems such as the hundreds of contradictions in the Bible; the lack of any of the original manuscripts that are supposed to have been inspired; how to translate and interpret them so that infallibility is preserved, and so on.

The differences between liberals and conservative evangelicals need to be assessed carefully. Liberals will want to *conserve* everything in the Bible and Tradition that speaks compellingly of Christ, and either to revise or to abandon altogether those things that do not. Liberals also joyfully proclaim the Gospel, or *euaggelion*. Their differences with conservative evangelicals are principally about what the Bible is and how it should be read, and these affect everything else.

Conservative evangelicals call the Bible 'the Word of God'. This is curious, for the Bible is very clear that *Jesus Christ* is the Word of God (John 1.14), and *not* 'the scriptures' (John 5.39). They treat the literal sense of Scripture as normative wherever possible. This way of reading Scripture was new at the Reformation, and has been retained by large sections of Protestantism ever since. These unfortunate suppositions lead conservative evangelicals to suppose that the Bible can be read as a guidebook for Christian living, especially in matters of personal morality. These handicaps make it almost impossible for them to make sense of sex. There are scores of cases in the First Testament where the requirements of property and purity laws seem to us primitive, disgusting and demeaning,[25] but, if the Bible is to be read literally, these passages are highly problematic for those Christians who seek guidance from them. Equally difficult are the many calumnies against womankind: for example, being condemned by an angry god to excruciating labour pains because of the disobedience of the first woman: 'I will greatly increase your pains in childbearing; with pain you will give birth to children' (Gen. 3.16). Forever subject to their husbands, submission and childbearing is their route to possible salvation (1 Tim. 2.15).

These Bible passages and many others are very difficult for evangelical Christians to deal with, and cause consternation among them. They seek to lead a holy life and to conform to the will of a holy God, yet the Bible gets in the way! Issues such as 'male headship' or the ministry of women cause bitter divisions among them. Often such passages are ignored or their interpretation forced to conform to a semblance of contemporary assumptions about gender equality. The problems don't end there. Evangelicals find in the Bible what isn't there. The story of Onan, who 'spilled his semen on the ground' (Gen. 38.9) was once used to condemn masturbation (perhaps it still is), yet it is about the failure to fulfil the obligations of an institution that Christianity has never recognized – Levirate marriage.

> Evangelicals find in the Bible what isn't there

Many liberals are Catholics, but liberals in the *Roman* Catholic Church are having a hard time since that Church lurched back into a rigid traditionalism following the liberalizing Second Vatican Council. Liberals often have a sense of the 'catholicity' (the worldwide scope) of Christ's Church, and a deep respect for the Catholic Tradition. It is conservative interpretations of the Tradition that they find difficult (which usually amount to leaving men in charge and everything else as it always allegedly was). There are plenty of issues where Catholics and liberals are at odds. Liberals think that the dogma of compulsory celibacy for priests is catastrophic, as is the denial of contraception to Catholics, whether married or not. These issues signal even greater fissures between Roman Catholics and Protestants, such as where authority lies in the Church's doctrinal and moral teaching.

What Liberal Theology is

Modern Church is well aware that 'liberal' has become a term of abuse. It is a casualty of relentless polemic. It has unfortunate associations with economics, where 'liberal' stands for free trade, the right of (wealthy) individuals to invest, and so for a market system that facilitates it. In politics, it is associated in Britain with the minority Liberal Party, which has its roots in the struggles of Protestant Nonconformists, for whom freedom of belief and the right to self-government in church matters were paramount. In theology, it is associated with a strand of thought known as Liberal Protestantism, which was influentially criticized by Karl Barth. Liberal Theology has also been overtaken by new currents in theology which, while drawing on many liberal principles, disguise the fount of ideas from which they spring. Whole movements in theology, like Radical Orthodoxy, Liberation Theology, Feminist Theology, even Postliberal Theology, all overlap with Liberal Theology even as they react to it or overtake it in impact in Church and world.

The place of Reason

Liberal Theology affirms all the sources of theology we have just considered, but gives a larger place to Reason than some other theologies do.[26] 'Reason' can mean 'argument', 'critical thinking', 'word', 'inquiry', and so on. The Greek word for reason is *logos*, 'word'. The appeal to reason is an insistence that the power of human thought is an integral step towards our apprehension and love of God. We have just referred to the commandment of Jesus himself to 'Love the Lord your God ... with all your mind'. Liberals affirm the belief in the power of the mind to arrive at new truths. They think that the power of mind is given by God, and that within its limits it can be trusted. Liberals have always welcomed new scientific knowledge. Knowledge about origins, whether it is the origin of the universe, of species, or even of the Scriptures themselves, are obvious examples. Reason does not *replace* Scripture, but is needed to interpret Scripture and to undertake the task of showing its relevance to contemporary faith and practice.

Liberal Theology stands in the mainstream of Christian theology in respecting and using the achievements of human inquiry as a source for thinking about God. Many great theologians have done this. Augustine (354–430) borrowed from Plato and the work of the Neo-Platonists. Aquinas (1225–74) was much influenced by Aristotle and the natural sciences of the time. All human knowledge that was not theology was once thought to be a type of philosophy – moral, natural, experimental, and so on. The contribution of Reason to our knowledge of sexuality is huge. Sexuality is studied by various academic disciplines (among them psychology, sociology, anthropology, philosophy and biology). The conclusions of these disciplines are generally provisional and contested, but they assist greatly in helping to understand the human sexual condition. Any assumption that we know it all already because we have the Bible turns out to be arrogant, ignorant and very dangerous.

> Liberal Theology stands in the mainstream of Christian theology in respecting and using the achievements of human inquiry as a source for thinking about God.

Liberal Theology is traditional, then, in its use of Reason. It shares two of its distinctive features with 'Revisionism',[27] another strand of contemporary theology. These are, first, 'that methodological problems need to be faced at the outset'. It asks what we want to know, and how to go about it. Second, it 'recognizes the importance and significance of modernity for theology'. That is because 'our texts were constructed in a pre-modern age. And the dramatic changes since the western Enlightenment need to be faced.'

> The dramatic changes since the western Enlightenment need to be faced

Individualism

Another strand of Liberal Theology which requires some justification is its affirmation of individualism. It is awkward for liberals to own up to this because 'individualism' has become associated with neglect of

Making sense of the sources

community, with selfishness, with consumerism. The 'me-generation', plugged in to iPods, iPads, iPhones and iTunes is an easy target for the charge of disconnectedness and an obsession with the latest technological microgadgetry. This is, of course, unfair. In Liberal Theology individuals are encouraged to make up their minds about what faith is, and how they are to apply it to their own lives. That is not to say that there are no boundaries to faith; it *is* to say that within those boundaries there is much scope for variety in individual belief and practice. Liberals and evangelicals actually share an adherence to individualism. Liberals make the obvious point that in order to accept the Faith one must at least begin to understand what one is accepting. Reason is needed for this to happen. Evangelicals stress the need for conversion, which requires the full response of the individual soul.

With this chapter the preliminaries have come to an end. We turn next to the issues.

2
Making sense of desire – from repression to expression

In this chapter the problem that sexual desire poses for people of faith is addressed. Some of the dire warnings against desire and its expression, found in Scripture and Tradition, are noted, and an explanation is offered for why Christian thought became 'sex-negative'. Some of the historical consequences of sex-negative teachings are outlined. A 'sex-positive' approach to desire and sexual experience, based on the sources discussed in Chapter 1, is then offered. Use of these, together with an openness to different scriptures, provides a different and positive perspective upon desire. In Chapter 3 desire and the body will be rooted in Christian *doctrine*, and this will be shown to provide a convincing framework within which to locate our sexual lives.

The problem of desire

Desire seems to be amply condemned in the Second Testament. There are 30 references to the evil of 'fornication'.[1] Even marriage is discouraged in some places (Luke 20.34–36; 1 Cor. 7.8–9, 25–38). A scholarly dispute continues over whether Paul condemned *all* sexual desire whatsoever, even within marriage, or whether his condemnation extended only to sinful, distorted or misdirected desire. On the former view, marriage is given not as a means to *indulge* desire, but to bring desire to an end.[2] Yes, sex within marriage must be 'passionless',[3] as close to celibacy as possible if celibacy cannot be achieved. The more moderate view is that Paul, in harmony with almost all Jewish, Greek and Roman literature of the period, did not condemn 'sexual desire *per se*' but rather 'sexual immorality (in various forms) and overpowering, excessive, or misdirected desire'.[4]

Making sense of desire

More straightforwardly, Paul seemed to regard sin as an impersonal, external force that controlled the human person by inhabiting the body and requiring obedience to evil desires (Rom. 6.12). Rather, Christians are now 'slaves to righteousness' (Rom. 6.18). The Spirit and 'the desires of the flesh' are sometimes depicted as locked in conflict, choosing individual Christians as their battleground (Gal. 5.16–21). There are similar warnings in most of the Second Testament Letters (for example, Eph. 5.3; Col. 3.5; 1 Pet. 4.3–4; 1 John 2.15–16). The authors of 2 Peter and Jude use the language of lust as a swingeing metaphor against their doctrinal opponents (2 Pet. 2.18–19; Jude 16, 18). This is an uncharitable characterization of some Christians by other Christians, and probably indicates a troublesome, feverish attitude to sexuality and the body.[5]

Modern readers may be able to take all this in their stride. The stark contrasts between spirit and flesh, purity and impurity, sin and righteousness, and so on, may be taken as battle-lines or 'polar-opposites' which, in real life, are more blurred and nuanced. Our biggest problem in reading the Second Testament is that scholars seem to agree about almost nothing. Does Paul think that all sexual desire is to be extirpated? Or is William Loader right in holding that 'the NT writers are one in seeing sex as belonging to God's creation and so as being a natural part of life to be enjoyed in the right place and the right time'?[6] We can, however, be clear that as the first century drew to a close, the churches (or at any rate their theologians) became increasingly fearful of sexual desire and more censorious towards all sexual behaviour, including even the enjoyment of marital sex. The influence of biblical injunctions thought to advocate celibacy (Matt. 19.11–12; Luke 20.34–36), together with Paul's ambivalence over marriage, and the reaffirmation of ancient patterns of gendered relations between men and women, led to a troublesome and problematic relationship between the Church and the sexuality of its members, which has remained ever since. In the time of Augustine (354–430), Jovinian (d. 405) was vilified and condemned for continuing to hold the historical position that celibacy and marriage were both of equal value. Augustine's work, *On the Goods of Marriage*, was an attempt to mediate between Jerome (347–420), who was contemptuous towards Paul's reluctant acceptance of marriage, and Jovinian, one of the few to defend what had once been a traditional view.[7] But Augustine's view of sex, that it was always sinful (though in marriage sometimes excusable) and indeed the purveyor of the original sin of Adam and Eve, came to dominate the Western Tradition for over a thousand years. Augustine's influence over Christian theologies of sex remains powerful.

> Augustine's influence over Christian theologies of sex remains powerful

Why Christianity became sex-negative

Why did the Christian tradition become 'sex-negative'? What were the consequences? How are we to read it for ourselves now? In response to the first question, here are three answers. First, Paul's preference for celibacy over marriage really did make marriage seem second best, so that Christians intent on achieving the kind of holy life that they saw most pleasing to God felt obliged to renounce sexual feelings and relationships. Peter Brown observes that 1 Corinthians 7 lacks 'the warm faith shown by contemporary pagans and Jews that the sexual urge, although disorderly, was capable of socialization and of ordered, even warm, expression within marriage'. This lack 'left a fatal legacy to future ages', while Paul's nuanced arguments

> slid imperceptibly into an attitude that viewed marriage itself as no more than a defence against desire. In the future, a sense of the presence of 'Satan', in the form of a constant and ill-defined risk of lust, lay like a heavy shadow in the corner of every Christian church.[8]

Second, the male leaders of the early Church believed that the bodies of women were a source of temptation, and of physical and moral pollution. There was ample biblical support for this view. These same bodies were also desired (and desiring), so it became necessary to require them to be dressed modestly (1 Pet. 3.1–6) and to be controlled at all times. The male fear of women's bodies, and of having sex with them, is exemplified in Revelation, where the 144,000 elect are identified as 'those who did not defile themselves with women, for they kept themselves pure. They follow the Lamb wherever he goes' (Rev. 14.4). That verse comes close to outright misogyny.

Did not the man have priority over the woman because he was created first? Was it not Eve, and not Adam, who was responsible for the ruination of humankind? Was it not the man, and not the woman, who alone was created in the image of God? Was she not created for the man's sake? Were not women to be saved (but only conditionally) 'through childbearing – if they continue in faith, love and holiness with propriety' (1 Tim. 2.15; cf. 1 Cor. 11.8–10)? While these and other texts reflect standard rabbinic teaching and standard gender assumptions of the time and are usually accompanied today by compensatory remarks (that rightly inflame Christian feminists today), it is easy to see how subsequent generations of Christians read them.

> These and other texts reflect standard rabbinic teaching and standard gender assumptions of the time

Third, Christians in the Roman Empire found the surrounding culture influenced by Stoicism. Three emphases of this widespread philosophy of life were *apatheia* or 'passionlessness'; the use of 'logos' or 'reason'; and (closely related to reason) the need for order or control. Influential Christian theologians largely agreed with these emphases. They recognized that Stoics mistrusted passion and emotion, and they admired them for it. That is why Paul is read as advocating *apatheia*.[9] While the priority of reason over emotion in natural law, and in ethics generally, has led to philosophical rigour, it has decimated the place of passion and what for the last 20 years has been called

> Stoics mistrusted passion and emotion

'emotional intelligence' in the moral and religious life. This weakness remains sadly unaddressed in much sexual ethics, even today.

The elevation of Reason requires the achievement of *order* in the political, social and moral worlds. For men, this required control of their women, and for householders it required control of their households. But now the great psychological problem arises. A man would be ridiculed if he could not control his household. Yet control was thought to begin with a man's own emotions and desires. If he could not control these he hardly counted as a man. Yet we have learned that the complete rational control of emotions is likely to be difficult or even impossible for many of us. To the extent that we are successful at it, we may actually lose emotional warmth and the possibility of positive relationships with other people. Indeed, there are many

> There are many controlled males around who have bought some level of control to their lives at the expense of moral and emotional self-harm

controlled males around who have bought some level of control to their lives at the expense of moral and emotional self-harm. They may even be a danger to other people when the tension between reason and passion causes them to split apart. It is hard to see how these lives are pleasing to God or anyone else, including themselves.

Let us note in passing how evangelical Christians today are in painful disarray about what to do with texts like the ones just cited. There seem to be four options, but only one is workable. First, they can under-emphasize them, ignore them, or pretend that they are not there. That doesn't work because on an evangelical view, these passages, like all the others, constitute the Word of God, so they must be heard. Second, they can act on them. That leaves male power intact, but is deeply unattractive and unjust. What self-respecting Christian man wants a submissive wife? What pointless privations are inflicted on the Church by excluding women from ministry (and in the Catholic case administering the sacraments)? Third, they can try to reconcile these passages with a more contemporary understanding of gender (talking up such verses as Galatians 3.28 – 'neither . . . male nor female'), yet this requires an inexcusable mis-reading of texts, wrenched from their contexts. Or they can recognize that the gospel message has to be disentangled from ancient cultural norms. That is, of course, the right answer, but maintaining it makes them appear dangerously liberal!

The battle with *eròs*

There are serious consequences for Church and society arising from Christianity's battle with *eròs*. First, the sexualization of desire eclipses other objects of desire and leaves them unremarked. 'This narrow construal of desire leaves largely unchallenged the relentless shaping of desires by the marketplace and communicates instead an uneasy, time-worn suspicion of desire as dangerous.'[10] The 'deadly sins' of greed, envy and gluttony, all of them fuelled by desire, are overlooked in the fascination with sexual desire, yet these same sins cause utter havoc in personal and global economic life. Second, the blatant exposure of the 'beautiful', stereotypical female body in social space and an increase in promiscuous sexual behaviour may both be the inevitable responses to earlier, unacceptable social norms that controlled what people wore and what they did. Third, the male attempt to hide the female body (a key element of several religious traditions) actually intensifies it as an object of desire by its very concealment. Its pornographic exposure may be a product of the fascination with what is denied.

Fourth, there is in many church congregations a huge problem of *sexual shame*. A useful definition of shame is 'an inner sense of being completely diminished or insufficient as a person'.[11] A sexually shamed person has a recurring additional problem: there is 'a renewed experience of shame whenever he or she feels sexual excitement or considers sexual action'.[12] Karen McClintock has studied sexual shame in the churches, and claims that their general silence about sexual matters, together with selective condemnation of certain sexual behaviours, is an expression of their own corporate sexual shame.[13] She (and several other writers) claims that male-dominated Christianity has 'oversexualized' women,[14] and this oversexualization has infected the secular culture that has grown out of it. She finds that young people's difficulties with the churches and their teachings about sex have as much, if not more, to do with the embarrassment and unspoken rules surrounding sex, than with the overt teachings themselves, implausible though these are.

Fifth, untold damage can be done to the souls of men caught up in a patriarchal system that tries to control everything and everyone. Peter Black states that a sexual ethic based on control is likely to 'subdue its adherers so that they become fearful, passive, secretive, uncreative, and passionless'. Such traits, he explains, are 'the signs of the victims of erotized [sic] power'.[15] He makes a further, chilling suggestion that male victims of this sexual ethic are condemned to deriving sexual pleasure from the very attitudes and practices that they find deplorable in others:

> Of course, it is not difficult to embrace such a restrictive ethic if one accepts either the premise that being controlled is better than running the risk of letting desire and longing and even justice get out of control, or if one accepts the conviction that controlling is the ultimate pleasure of our desiring anyway, even though such pleasure needs to be vested with religious sentiment or outrightly denied.[16]

Rowan Williams shows how desire can only be satisfied if the attempt to control the object of our desire is abandoned. Rather it is in the *loss* of control that satiation occurs. While this may be hard for the patriarchal mind to entertain, it is a necessary feature of *mutual* sexual relations that desiring and being desired belong together: 'in sexual relation I am no longer in charge of what I am', says Williams, pointing out the difference between shared and auto-erotic experiences:

> For my body to be the cause of joy, the end of homecoming, for me, it must be there for someone else, must be perceived, accepted, nurtured. And that means being given over to the creation of joy in that other, because only as directed to the enjoyment, the happiness, of the other does it become unreservedly lovable.[17]

Owning our desires

This kind of controlling sexual ethic cannot help us today. If we wish to remain faithful Christians we may have to be 'loyal dissenters' from some biblical, and much traditional, teaching about sex and gender. What, then, are we to do if we discover that some biblical, and much traditional, teaching actually demeans half the human race, and gnaws away at our deepest longings for connection and fulfilment, negating them? The problem is not as difficult as it seems. We can easily find different Scriptures that treat desire differently; indeed we can dissociate ourselves altogether from quarrying the Scriptures for proof-texts that appear to give precise guidance about sexual matters beyond general principles. We can allow different Scriptures that are not sex-negative to impact upon us. Indeed, we can read the whole Bible differently, as a *witness* to God's Revelation in Christ, not as a moral guidebook.[18] We can understand Tradition as provisional and developing. We are not bound by it. We are bound instead to be tradition-makers ourselves, reworking it so that the challenge of faith is not rendered impossible by fossilized versions of it. We can *expect* the Tradition to change as the Church learns more of the fullness of Christ through the centuries. We can

> We may have to be 'loyal dissenters' from some biblical, and much traditional, teaching

Making sense of desire

bring the other sources into play (that were noted in Chapter 1). In the rest of this chapter we will do all these things, and arrive at a very different evaluation of desire.

The raging flame of passion

The Song of Songs is a collection of erotic poems that celebrates the desire of two young unmarried people for one another.[19] There are no anxious worries about desire here, no efforts at patriarchal control, no privileging of male experience, and not a word about making babies. Ever since the Songs were compiled, an allegorical reading has been preferred, with the result that readers' attention is directed away from the joy of sexual love that the Songs celebrate, into something much more abstract, like God's love for Israel or Christ's love for his Church. Readers' bodily engagement with the text (and possible arousal by it) is soon deflated. But at least the allegorical readers did something with the Song; modern biblicists have no use for it at all. It contains no moral guidance or sexual rules and so does not fit the rule-book attitude to the Bible. Biblicists consider the Song off-limits and dangerous, best read (if at all) in translations that obscure the rich, uninhibited eroticism that contrasts strikingly with casual attitudes to sex and the objectification of the body in our own time. Worse, the whole book contains no direct reference to God! However, the man tells his lover:

> Set me as a seal upon your heart,
> as a seal upon your arm;
> for love is strong as death,
> passion fierce as the grave.
> Its flashes are flashes of fire,
> a raging flame.   (Song of Songs 8.6)[20]

The last syllable of the Hebrew word for 'blaze' or 'flame' is *yah*, and *yah* is 'a shortened form of Israel's personal name for God'. The 'raging flame' or 'all-consuming blaze' is also 'the flame of Yah: divinity is the measure of the intensity of eros'.[21] Yes, there are references to God in the Song after all. God is the fire of the fiery passion between the lovers. And God is the 'artist' or 'craftsman'[22] who has delightfully crafted the girl's 'graceful legs' (Song of Songs 7.1, NIV) or 'the curves' of her 'thighs' (REB).

Making sense of desire

Intoxicated love

Proverbs 1—9 also provides a positive account of desire. It is an attempt by a parent to give instruction to a child. These chapters actually place an 'extraordinary emphasis' on desire.[23] Yoder notes how in these chapters, 'Desire itself is assumed; the concern is the power of desire rightly or wrongly directed.' There are clearly right and wrong objects of desire, as the following verses show:

> May your fountain be blessed,
> and may you rejoice in the wife of your youth.
> A loving doe, a graceful deer –
> may her breasts satisfy you always,
> may you ever be captivated by her love.
> Why be captivated, my son, by an adulteress?
> Why embrace the bosom of another man's wife? (Prov. 5.18–20)

There is here an honest recognition of desire, and a delight in the body of a partner, far from Augustine's prim advice that ageing married couples should give up having sex as soon as possible.[24] This paternal teacher of wisdom knows that 'the pursuit and attainment of knowledge is not about the extirpation of passion. Rather, it requires cultivation of it.'[25] Yes, sustaining passion in a marriage becomes an imperative – and the best of reasons for sticking together. In the previous chapter we included Wisdom among the sources for making sense of sex. Wisdom is repeatedly associated in Proverbs with the love and fidelity of spouses, while its opposite, 'folly', is associated with adultery and capitulation to temptation.

Sex and self-love

Christian sexual ethics should take the core doctrine that 'God is love' (1 John 4.8, 16) much more seriously. *Eròs*, or desire, is a component of love. Sexual ethics is a developed form of neighbour-love that resides in the divine love that God is. *Ubi caritas ibi deus est* ('where there is love, there is God'). This neighbour-love is informed and shaped by the divine love that reaches out towards everyone. It is more a matter of *relation* than prescription. There is a much-neglected feature of neighbour-love – it is co-related to *self-love*.[26] We are enjoined to love our neighbours, not more or less than our love for ourselves, but *as* ourselves. Self-love too is a requirement, not a temptation to be resisted in the name of self-sacrifice. To be a loving neighbour one needs to be at peace with oneself. There has to be positive self-affirmation in fulfilling these commandments. Too often, rigorous sexual prescriptions have led away from self-love to self-hatred. This is a particular problem for women, and the Christian tradition is partly responsible, for, as Julie Rubio rightly observes, it 'is better at insisting on the sin of self-indulgence than the sin of failing in self-love, and women are particularly adept at taking this message to heart'.[27]

> To be a loving neighbour one needs to be at peace with oneself

Rereading the sources

The Second Testament Letters depict their authors reflecting theologically on their own faith and that of their recipients, and offering advice about how to live it out in practical ways that distinguished Christian communities from the surrounding pagan culture. The Letters *witness* to a developing faith. They do not provide a finished product. Christian faith today must make its witness in a very different social and sexual environment. The patristic period is governed by gender-assumptions. We think that these assumptions, like those about slavery, are ultimately contrary to the freedom and self-worth that the gospel bestows on all people, men and women. Two of these assumptions were that men controlled women, and that in order to do so they first needed to be able to control themselves. But suppose that in sexual relations we are not interested in control, but in self-abandonment? Suppose that sexual pleasure is one of the ways that God enables us to cement mutual love? Suppose that a greater sexual pleasure is the pleasure of our partner, and not the wresting of our own satisfaction in control? Suppose that love and joy, the first two of the fruits of the Spirit (Gal. 5.22) are known primarily in bodily intimacy – the kiss, the embrace, the cuddle?

> Christian faith today must make its witness in a very different social and sexual environment

Sometimes Christians honour Tradition by changing it. We do not have to keep on repeating it, especially when keeping it as it was leads to ghastly results. We are honour-bound to *change* it whenever it is morally inadequate. We are Tradition-makers as well as Tradition-upholders. This side of eternity all our knowledge is provisional, and therefore revisable in the light of new insights and experiences that God may give us.

> We are Tradition-makers as well as Tradition-upholders

The use of Reason leads to a similar conclusion. Reason can be cold, impersonal, detached and controlling. Its exercise, on such a view, must be able to check emotion, which because it is warm, personal, involved and affirming is also thought to be fickle and unreliable. That provides a further reason for Reason to control it. But Reason can join with emotion, not battle with it. There can be no moral knowledge worth having without empathy or involvement. Reason need not repress emotion (as in Stoicism). It can help to bring about emotional maturity.

Two kinds of ecstasy?

Experience is also able to guide us. Clearly there is no experience in the abstract: there are only experiences *of* something or someone. Experiences of desire never happen in the abstract: always there is an object, and with sexual desire that object is a person. Generally, there are no experiences that come to us 'raw', as it were, uninterpreted by language. Perhaps, though, there are particularly intense experiences that so overwhelm consciousness that, temporarily, awareness of the source is blocked out. Here is a fragment of Mary Pellauer's candid description of having an orgasm with her partner:

> If I am lucky, I do go over the edge. Tremors center in my pelvis, vibrating me like a violin string. As I am shaken from the hips outward, my bones turn to lava, languorous liquid fire, heated jelly in the pelvis and thighs, magma coursing molten down.[28]

It actually seems impossible for an experience of such an intense kind *not* to have a religious dimension, doesn't it? This is not to identify orgasmic experience with experience of the divine: it is to note that the orgasmic experience is both *ecstatic* and *mystical*, like the experience of God reported by countless religious mystics. It is to say that a whole range of common elements are present both in this frank sexual description and in the experience of men and women who stand in the mystical tradition of faith. Both dimensions are present as Pellauer continues:

> The orgasmic experience is both *ecstatic* and *mystical*, like the experience of God reported by countless religious mystics

> At the moment/eternity of orgasm itself, I melt into existence and it melts into me. I am most fully embodied in this explosion of nerves and also broken open into the cosmos. I am rent open; I am cleaved/joined not only to my partner, but to everything, everything-as-my-beloved (or vice versa), who has also become me.

The joy of sex

Rowan Williams has noticed that, within the wisdom of God, our desires do not always coincide with the task of having children.[29] The justification for having sex with a married partner was that children might result (and, of course, avoiding fornication). However, if this justification is the only one, then not only same-sex love but most straight sex too does not and cannot be considered legitimate. A problem with this justification is that it is *instrumental*: having sex is a means towards having something else – children. But suppose the meaning of desire is not at all exhausted by the purpose of having children? Perhaps the meaning of desire is gratuitous, 'non-functional joy'? He continues:

> The question is the same as the one raised . . . by the existence of the clitoris in women: something whose function is joy. If the Creator were quite so instrumentalist in 'his' attitude to sexuality, these hints of prodigality and redundancy in the way the whole thing works might cause us to worry about whether 'he' was, after all, in full rational control of it. But if God made us for joy?

There is a whole raft of insights in this dense half-paragraph. First, God has equipped us for *joyful* sex, not just reproductive sex. Second, God is no instrumentalist, giving us the required bits to make babies, and limiting our sexual faculties to their single allotted task.

That would require us having different bodies from the ones we have. Third, not even God exercises control over sexuality in the manner to which the Stoics or the Roman Catholic Church aspire to control it. Fourth, the wasteful extravagance ('prodigality') and superfluous overlapping ('redundancy') of our sexual faculties may indicate more of the Creator's will in making us joyful, or, as Williams says, 'embodied person[s] aware of grace'.

The intensity of orgasmic experience is partly responsible for the insatiable desire for it (which is not to say that it is always necessary for having fulfilling sex). The desire for union with an 'other' can be unbearably strong. That is, in the end, one of the reasons why the Christian faith is rightly wary of desire, because it lies at the root of much personal behaviour that is destructive and sinful. It lies at the root of envy and gluttony. Acquisitiveness is carefully cultivated by corporate institutions and finance houses, and may ultimately be the ruination of the capitalist economic system. Sexual desire wrongly directed or entirely uncontrolled is certain to have negative consequences. It can demean people, and it has brought millions of unwanted children into the world. Adulterous desire almost always brings unhappiness, and to act upon it is wrong (even though our sense of its 'wrongness' will be very different from the ancient belief that it is a sin against a married man to violate his uxorial property, that is, his wife). The problem for Christian sexual ethics is that for many people on the fringe of or outside the Church, we have become besotted with sex, and the rows about homosexuality appear to be the final desperate attempts of a Church that has almost completely lost its influence to control what people choose to do with their lives.

Sexual desire can lead us away from God: to selfishness, to exploitation of the other, to deceit, to reducing persons to objects. But (and this point is generally missed), sexual desire can *lead us to God*. It can drive us out of ourselves to seek connection with a beloved other, and in seeking and making this connection we may also connect with another beloved Other who infinitely desires us. We probe more deeply into the divine love in the next chapter.

3

Making sense of bodies – from 'sinful bodies' to the Body of Christ

In this chapter sexual love is placed within the Christian doctrinal framework that makes sense of it. In the first section, a clear path is laid between God's love and human sexual love. Strong connections are made between our being made in the image of God and our being-in-relation to other people and to God. In the second part of the chapter, sense is made of human bodies by linking them with the Body of Christ. The Eucharist will be shown to be essential for understanding and transforming both sexuality and sexual love. The chapter contrasts the created goodness of the body with the body-negativity that can still be found in some Christian thought.

Sexual love and divine love

Pope Benedict's recent reflections on love provide a useful entry into the subject. Benedict admits that 'Nowadays Christianity of the past is often criticized as having been opposed to the body; and it is quite true that tendencies of this sort have always existed.'[1] He does not admit that Christianity of the *present* is paying a high price for its past opposition to the body, not least the large-scale abandonment of the faith by once-Christian people who are bemused by archaic Christian teachings about the body and sexuality. Benedict continues:

> Yet the contemporary way of exalting the body is deceptive. *Eros*, reduced to pure 'sex', has become a commodity, a mere 'thing' to be bought and sold, or rather, man himself becomes a commodity. This is hardly man's great 'yes' to the body. On the contrary, he now considers his body and his sexuality as the purely material part of himself, to be used and exploited at will.

Making sense of bodies

Benedict's analysis relies on three familiar Greek concepts of love – *agapè*, *eròs* and *philia*[2] – and an integrated view of the individual person. First, love. *Eròs*, he says, is 'that love between man and woman which is neither planned nor willed, but somehow imposes itself on human beings'.[3] It does not appear in the Second Testament. *Philia*, 'the love of friendship ... is used with added depth of meaning in Saint John's Gospel in order to express the relationship between Jesus and his disciples'. *Agapè* in the Second Testament expresses 'the new vision of love'. It points to 'something new and distinct about the Christian understanding of love'. There is 'an intrinsic link between that Love and the reality of human love'.[4] '*Eros* and *agape* – ascending love and descending love – can never be completely separated. The more the two, in their different aspects, find a proper unity in the one reality of love, the more the true nature of love in general is realized.'[5]

Next, the human person. Benedict follows the moderate view of Aquinas that a person is an *integrated* union of body and soul. Body and soul are not separate entities or substances (as they are for Plato and Descartes). They belong together in the unity of the person, and that unity is disrupted when either one is emphasized at the expense of the other. Clinging to his disconcertingly exclusive language, Benedict observes: 'Man is truly himself when his body and soul are intimately united.' The problem for humanity is that *eròs* disrupts the unity. Two contrasting responses to the disruption of *eròs* are then described. One is to 'aspire to be pure spirit and to reject the flesh as pertaining to his animal nature alone'. The result is that 'spirit and body would both lose their dignity'. The other response is the denial of spirit and affirmation of the body 'as the only reality'. While Benedict does not admit that the first response is pretty accurately what much Christianity has in fact tried to do, he is convinced that the second response provides an accurate diagnosis of the contemporary experience of sexual love.

Lovers in the image of God

Although Benedict is a highly conservative theologian in matters of sexuality, I have no quarrel (apart from the exclusive language) with his descriptions of love. However, since we are examining love specifically in sexual relationships, I think there may be a better way of making the 'intrinsic link' between 'ascending love' and 'descending love' more explicit. That way is through the doctrine of the Trinity and the belief that humankind is made in the image of God (*imago dei*). Christians are unanimous that human beings are made in God's image:

> Then God said, 'Let us make man in our image, in our likeness, and let them rule over the fish of the sea and the birds of the air, over the livestock, over all the earth, and over all the creatures that move along the ground.'
>
> So God created man in his own image,
> in the image of God he created him;
> male and female he created them. (Gen. 1.26–27)

The problem, of course, is *how* humans image God: what aspects of the divine are mirrored in the human? Something in us is an icon of God, but what? *Reason* has been the prime candidate in the West. Sibley Towner has a list of ten types of answers to the question,[6] all of them used in Christian thought, past and present. However, there is a growing tendency to reject a one-to-one correspondence between properties shared between God and people, and to understand the *imago dei* instead as *relations of love* between people.[7] 'Mankind' is a society, not an individual, and 'mankind' is sexed (what to make of 'male and female he created them' must be postponed until Chapter 4). God is, of course, in Christian thought a Trinity of Persons, and these Persons, too, are in relation. How human persons image the divine Persons is in their relations with one another.

> What aspects of the divine are mirrored in the human? Something in us is an icon of God, but what?

It is not assumed that the writer of Genesis 1 had any inkling about the Trinity. The plural 'Let us . . .' is more likely to reflect an earlier belief that God had a consort, or at least consorted with a panoply of lesser gods in making humanity (monotheism was slow to arrive in the First Testament). It is more important for Christians to understand that Christ is the image of God (Col. 1.15) than to speculate about the possible meanings of Gen. 1.27. However, Christian thought about the nature of humanity continues to be greatly indebted to this

> Human beings are made for *communion*, and in this respect they image the God who *is* Communion

text. God is Love. God is three Persons. Yet God is one – the Persons are always distinct yet always united. The Persons are 'Persons-in-relation'. Now human persons find themselves in the image of God: that is, in the image of the divine Persons. Human beings are made for *communion*, and in this respect they image the God who *is* Communion, the Communion of Persons.

This is now an official teaching of the Roman Catholic Church, and marriage is the supreme instance of it. Beginning with a Second Vatican Council document,[8] and further developed by Pope John Paul II, the Church teaches that 'The image of God, which is to be found in the nature of the human person as such, can be realized in a special way in the union between human beings.' While admitting that 'union between human beings can be realized in a variety of ways', according to a recent document (completed in 2002),

> Catholic theology today affirms that marriage constitutes an elevated form of the communion between human persons and one of the best analogies of the Trinitarian life. When a man and a woman unite their bodies and spirits in an attitude of total openness and self-giving, they form a new image of God.[9]

Love is a relation

In several places over many years, I have been calling love a *relation*.[10] This might seem unhelpfully abstract, but its significance is considerable. The renewed emphasis in philosophy on the person as a person-in-relation in the third quarter of the twentieth century,[11] assisted in the renascence of the doctrine of the social Trinity in the final quarter. I am awaiting a similar transformation of the *concept of love*: that is, from love as a property belonging to a subject, to love as the quality of a relation *between* human subjects.

> Love as the quality of a relation *between* human subjects

Within the diverse interpretations of love in Christian thought there is likely to be agreement that, first and foremost, love is the property or quality of a subject, human or divine. It is often described as an 'attitude'. As such it has a subject, the self or agent who expresses the attitude, and an object of the attitude. As an attitude it is a property of an agent who displays it in his or her actions. On this view, love becomes the supreme Christian attitude, a *virtue* that we realize fully only with the help of God. The difficulty I am raising with this basic understanding of love is not that it is wrong, but that it is one-sided, and that the other side is rarely put. The alternative approach to love is as a relation, where both lover and beloved are equally subject, and love is the relation between them. Balance may be restored to Christian treatments of the concept of love by seeing love as a *quality* of the relation between the lover and who or what is loved.

On this view God is not just a single divine Subject or Individual, who possesses the virtue of love supremely, and in whose image individuals are made. The communion of the Three suggests a different picture. God *is* Love, and the Relations within God constitute the divine Communion. Human relations are offered a participation in the divine Relations. There are fairly obvious links to be pursued between this, the social model of the Trinity, the relational concept of the person or self,[12] and the understanding of love as the potential dynamics of all personal relations.

The relational concept of love applies to God and to ourselves. God is no 'Individual with attitude': rather, God is the mutual love of Persons for one another in a Communion where each is also distinct. That is how we image God. The relational concept of love restores to love the primacy that properly belongs to it. If love is an attitude or a virtue,

> God is the mutual love of Persons for one another in a Communion where each is also distinct

belonging to an individual subject, then it is a property of an individual. The individual is clearly primary – the subject with the property. If love is a relation, then *love* is primary, embracing both subjects.

Learning about God through sexual love

In this section we have thought about God the Trinity, about the image of God, and about the nature of love. The connexion between these deep truths of faith and a Christian sex life should by now have become clear. As Todd Salzman and Michael Lawler say:

> The act of sexual intercourse allows humans a unique insight into the love shared within the Trinity. In intercourse there is the unconditional gift of self to the other and the unconditional reception of the other's gift of self in return. Such mutuality, reciprocity, and unconditional acceptance reflect the total self-surrender within the Trinity... The love, including the sexual love, shared by a couple in relationship draws them together into communion, and this shared communion reflects the communion of the Trinity.[13]

Not all sex, of course, is like this. Sex can be exploitative and depersonalizing (as Salzman and Lawler readily acknowledge). Yet here is to be found a remarkable introduction to the core concepts of faith actually in and through the practices of love-making. But is not such love-making confined to the sacrament of marriage alone? While the easy (and very preliminary) answer to that question is 'Yes, of course', the more interesting question is why marriage was ever made into a sacrament at all. One interesting answer is because marital sex really does convey these meanings: 'the communion between spouses expressed in the sexual intercourse that characterizes marriage is also a sacrament of the divine communion. That, of course, is precisely what the Catholic Church intends when it teaches that marriage is a sacrament.'[14]

> **The communion between spouses expressed in the sexual intercourse that characterizes marriage is also a sacrament of the divine communion**

The Christian faith is, in one sense, deeply materialistic. It holds that God became revealed in the *flesh* of Christ: the term 'in*carn*ation' means 'enfleshment' (from the Latin *carnis*, 'flesh'). There could hardly be a more jarring identification between the divine and the human than this. Yet 'carnal' is generally identified with 'carnal sins' ('the sins of the flesh'), and 'the flesh' in the Second Testament, as we have seen, is often contrasted with 'spirit' and made to stand for sinful human nature separated from God (for example, Romans 8.1–12). But the Greek word *sarx* ('flesh') is capable of being given widely different meanings. Paul used the term more than 91 times in his letters.[15] The temptation to synthesize all these meanings should be resisted. Christians mean different things by 'flesh'. One of these meanings is incredibly positive. Flesh is what God became. Flesh is capable of receiving and embodying the divine.

Bodies and the Body of Christ

So far the doctrines of Trinity and the *imago dei* have shaped the discussion of sexuality and the body. The rest of the chapter allows Christian beliefs about the Body of Christ to reshape our understanding of our bodies. The Body of Christ has several senses in the Second Testament. Two only will be selected. The first is that of the Body of Christ as Church, which comprises all its members (Rom. 13.5). It is what Paul meant when he concluded, 'Now you are the body of Christ, and each one of you is a part of it' (1 Cor. 12.27). The second meaning is that of the Body of Christ as *bread* – what is given and received at the Eucharist. Both of these have far-reaching implications for sexuality.

Fields of communication

What is it to have and to be a body? We have already seen that to be a person is to be in relation. Anthony Kelly explains how this works at the embodied level:

> My body is not merely something I possess, but is rather the field of my communication with the other. The body or 'flesh' intimately constitutes the subject's being in the world. It implies possibilities of intimate self-giving and self-disclosure, as in the case of erotic or maternal love. In this sense, the flesh, our incarnate consciousness, is a field of mutual indwelling, of being with and for the other. In the eros and generativity of love, one's bodily being is re-experienced in, with, and through the flesh of the other.[16]

The idea of a 'field of communication' expresses well how 'I' am more than an item in a material world. Rather, through my body 'I' am in 'a field of conscious interactions, a zone of incarnated relationships'. 'My body', he says, 'is affected by the encompassing phenomenon of the world and in turn affects it. It is at once an elemental bonding with the world, an immediate exposure to it, an immediate participation in it, and a primal communication within it.'

Now the Body of Christ in the Second Testament is also a 'field of interaction', a 'field of communication'. 'Body of Christ' was a favourite metaphor for Paul, indeed more than a metaphor. It was an experienced reality, as well as a key element in his theology. In the following passage he assumes that individual believers are members of this one Body of Christ, and he then builds an argument based on this idea about who [not] to have sex with:

> Do you not know that your bodies are members of Christ himself? Shall I then take the members of Christ and unite them with a prostitute? Never! Do you not know that he who unites himself with a prostitute is one with her in body? For it is said, 'The two will become one flesh.' But whoever is united with the Lord is one with him in spirit.
>
> Flee from sexual immorality. All other sins a person commits are outside the body, but whoever sins sexually, sins against their own body. Do you not know that your bodies are temples of the Holy Spirit, who is in you, whom you have received from God? You are not your own; you were bought at a price. Therefore honour God with your bodies. (1 Cor. 6.15–20)

The argument works by synecdoche. Synecdoche is a figure of speech in which a part is used for the whole, or the whole for a part. For Paul it is more than a figure of speech: he seems to have figured out that there was a mutual participation between Christ's Body and the bodies of Christians, and this participation was able to influence their sexual behaviour. Their bodies are 'members of Christ himself'. Given that the bodies of Christians are part of the Body of Christ, it follows that when these bodies are sexually joined with other bodies, the Body of Christ is joined with them as well. In the case of Christians paying for sex the logic of the argument leads Paul to an appalling conclusion. When the men at Corinth had sex with prostitutes, the Body of Christ had sex with them as well. (The physiological understanding prevailing in Paul's time, about sperm and ejaculation, added a horrifying realism to the blasphemous thought of the Body of Christ and the bodies of prostitutes being sexually joined.)[17]

What happens in a mixed marriage when one partner is a Christian and the other is not? It is a problem because one is a member of the Body of Christ and the other isn't, but sex is OK here because the two are regarded as 'one flesh'. Paul's answer is: 'The unbelieving husband has been sanctified through his wife, and the unbelieving wife has been sanctified through her believing husband. Otherwise your children would be unclean, but as it is, they are holy' (1 Corinthians 7.14). In Paul's eyes a man who is a member of the Body of Christ, and who has sex with a woman to whom he is not married who is not a member of the Body of Christ, might seem to defile the greater body of which he is part. But if they are married, Paul thinks, their marriage sanctifies their relationship and the sexual exchanges within it.

There is here a valuing of the body in these verses which is capable of informing, if not transforming, what we do with them, what we take into them and with whom we share them. First, if the body is 'the temple of the Holy Spirit' then it is fairly obviously to be regarded as a 'place of God's dwelling'. There may be a suggestion here that the bodies of Christians 'bought with a price' are to be contrasted with the bodies of prostitutes bought for money in temples.[18] Second, if the body of a Christian is located within the primary field of communication which is the Body of Christ, if it represents it and is animated by it, then that mystical location is certain to influence bodily practices. Such a belief would and should perhaps also influence other choices about what we take into our bodies. Drunkenness, gluttony, and the thrill-seeking exposure to excessive risks are all, along with sexual risk-taking, rendered theologically problematic by the belief that one's body is part of the Body of Christ.

The gift of a body

But it is in the *giving* of a body, in the Eucharist, that sexual meanings abound. Several writers have found the greatest significance for sexual ethics in the Eucharist, understood as the gift of a body. 'While they were eating, Jesus took bread, gave thanks and broke it, and gave it to his disciples, saying, "Take it; this is my body"' (Mark 14.22).

Christians understand this saying in different ways, yet they are in broad agreement that Christ, in dying on the cross, gave his body at least as the exemplification of God's love 'poured out for many' (Mark 14.24). Another of the books in this series makes sense of God's acts of 'atonement' and 'redemption'.[19] These are 'remembered' whenever the Mass is celebrated. Without specifying how the eucharistic bread is or becomes the Body of Christ, there are clear analogies waiting to be drawn between the love-feast of the Lord's Supper and love-making with one's partner. Christians may need to become more familiar with these analogies.

> There are clear analogies waiting to be drawn between the love-feast of the Lord's Supper and love-making with one's partner

Body language, human and divine

Below are three separate statements of some of the parallels waiting to be made between the divine love shared at the Eucharist and the sexual love shared with one's partner. This is the first:

> It is surely obvious to anyone who has the gift of their lover's body in love-making and the gift of Christ's body in the Eucharist that there are many unexplored parallels between these two life-sustaining, life-enhancing, life-creating activities. They engage all our senses, especially the less prominent ones of touch, taste and smell. They are both intensely joyful celebrations, each deeply satisfying. Yet both may also be covenanted pledges of love, richly symbolic, festive and liberating.[20]

Several parallels are suggested here, each grounded in the experiences of receiving Christ's body, and the body of one's partner. Timothy Radcliffe provides a second set of comparisons between the Eucharist and love-making. He makes a pressing case for allowing the experience of the Eucharist to inform all our loving.[21]

> One can best get a glimpse of the depth and beauty of sexuality by looking at the Last Supper. It teaches us what it means to give our bodies to other people. Sexuality also helps us to understand the Last Supper. So I will argue that we can best understand sexuality in the light of the Eucharist, and the Eucharist in the light of our sexuality.[22]

Making sense of bodies

Radcliffe draws on the basic fact that 'the human body is the basis of all communication',[23] utilizing all its senses as it communicates with other bodies. The idea is almost the same as the body as a 'field of communication' just discussed. In the human case, he continues, communication is enhanced by language. Sharing meals together as people, compared, say, with lions gorging themselves over a carcass, can be a deep kind of communication. When 'Jesus wished to establish the new covenant between God and humanity, he gathered the disciples for a meal ... Eating did not just become the ingestion of nutrition, but expressed the common life of divinity and humanity.' In love-making, bodies communicate:

> Sexual intercourse ... becomes a fundamental expression of how we are in communion with one another. It is not that we speak before or after having sex, though that matters. It is that sexual behaviour should be communicative. It should be expressive of who are the people involved. It is a way of speaking deeply.[24]

It follows that sexual love is not a matter of obeying rules. It is more about 'What does my behaviour say?'[25] This too is Rowan Williams'

> Jesus holds nothing back.
> He gives us his body

starting point: 'the moral question, I suspect, ought to be: How much do we want our sexual activity to communicate?'[26] Well, Jesus holds nothing back. He gives us his body. As Radcliffe observes:

> When he gave us his body, he was expressing the deepest meaning of what it is to be a body ... These words of the Last Supper take us to the heart of a sexual ethic. Sexuality is about communion; it speaks. And what it should express is mutual generosity, the giving and receiving of gifts.[27]

There is no space to follow the argument where Radcliffe takes it – seeing the Eucharist in the context of the betrayal of Jesus by Judas, the overcoming of domination and violence (and even death), and suggesting that sexual love is able to be the place where truthfulness is spoken, vulnerability is honoured, and domination is overcome by mutuality. Instead we will note a third treatment of the parallels between the Eucharist and love-making:

Body language as the language of love

In *The Sexual Person*, Salzman and Lawler develop a eucharistic theology of the body, also drawing on a similar approach to communication and language. 'Beyond verbal language there is body language, and beyond body language there is ritual language, symbolic actions filled with socially approved meanings.' We are reminded that

> 'This is my body given for you' is something that *lovers* say to one another in the act of intercourse. In both the Last Supper and the sex, the body and the person synonymous with it are vulnerable, even broken, but both body and person are given in love to the other, trusting that they will be received in love and handled with care.[28]

That is why, and how, couples having sex can 'express love, forgiveness, reconciliation, affirmation, and thanksgiving', and do so 'in the most profound and total way available to an embodied human being, namely, through the completely unmasked and therefore totally vulnerable body'.[29] Such an understanding of sexual communication is not confined to Christianity, yet Catholic theology is thought to bring a distinctive understanding to it:

> The central theological point here is a very Catholic one. The God incarnate in the Christ who gives his body in the Supper for the salvation of all is the same God incarnate in the lovers and their act of mutual self-giving for the salvation of their relationship. In Catholic theology, the one ritual is as sacramental of God as the other, which is why both are listed among the Catholic sacraments.[30]

These descriptions of love-making are sometimes dismissed as completely unrealistic, and even to add a burden of meaning to what is also a light-hearted and playful activity. This criticism is unfair. Sex does not need to be imbued with transcendental meaning every time people have it. But it is open to these meanings. It is not generally understood how positive Christian theology is able to be in its appreciation and encouragement of good sex. And these descriptions also suggest the distress and moral poverty that casual sexual encounters generally bring about where these factors do not come into play. Too often sex is marred precisely because it does not honour vulnerability, revel in mutuality, speak a language of love, or express joy, and so on. Whether good sex can only be enjoyed between a man and a woman within marriage is discussed in Chapters 5 and 6.

4

Making sense of sexual difference – from difference to indifference

In this chapter, sexual difference is placed within the Christian doctrinal framework that helps to make sense of it. There are three 'differences' to be explored: the *biological* difference between male and female; the *gender* difference between masculine and feminine; and the *'orientation'* difference between the desires of apparently heterosexual, bisexual and homosexual people. The first two of these are explored in this chapter. The arguments about homosexuality must be postponed to Chapter 5.

The different meanings of difference

Each of these three areas of difference has been thought to designate a permanent division between people. The subtitle of this chapter, 'from difference to indifference', indicates that recent thought, secular and religious, has moved away from an emphasis on difference, to something much better – an appreciation of our common humanity. People are *equal*, in the sense that they are all equally loved by God, and are all entitled to basic human goods and rights, but the striving for equality does not and should not overlook the many differences between people, not just sexual differences.

> Striving for equality does not and should not overlook the many differences between people, not just sexual differences

'Difference', too, has different meanings. One is the opposite of 'identity' or 'sameness'. Another is the opposite of 'indifference'. 'Indifference' has several meanings. One is 'couldn't care less' ('he was indifferent about going out tonight'); another is 'mediocre' ('the team performed indifferently'); another is 'secondary' or 'unimportant'. That is the sense 'indifference' has in the disputes among Anglicans and others at the present time, only they refer to it by the Greek word *adiaphora*, which the *Windsor Report*[1] defined as 'things which do not make a difference, matters regarded as non-essential, issues about which one can disagree without dividing the Church'.[2] This was potentially a fruitful way of handling disagreement: relegating it to secondary or non-essential status, but there were – alas! – different views about whether the disagreement about homosexuality was secondary or more fundamental. This chapter traces how some differences, which were thought to be fundamental and so were of great importance, turn out *not* to be fundamental and so of no great importance at all. That is what 'from difference to indifference' tries to convey. Differences of sex, gender and (in the next chapter) orientation will be shown to be unimportant. We should be able to relax and rejoice in them. Unfortunately that happy circumstance is still a long way off.

Different bodies? Different sexes?

According to a standard modern view there are two distinct sexes, male and female. Genesis 1.27 is thought to authorize this belief and to confirm it:

> So God created mankind in his own image,
> in the image of God he created him;
> male and female he created them.

Everyone knows that this key verse belongs to one of the two creation narratives in Genesis. Conservative writers make much of the 'fact' that God made humanity in two sexes. Male and female represent the divine order. Much is also made of the use of this text by Jesus himself. When opposing Jewish teaching about divorce, Jesus gets behind the law of Moses to an earlier time, 'at the beginning of creation' (Mark 10.6). Jesus cites Genesis 1.27, and immediately combines it with a quotation from the second creation narrative, at Genesis 2.24:

> '"For this reason a man will leave his father and mother and be united to his wife, and the two will become one flesh." So they are no longer two, but one flesh. Therefore what God has joined together, let man not separate.'   (Mark 10.7–8; see Matt. 19.5–6)

Making sense of sexual difference

There has been much discussion of the meaning of 'one flesh'. Sexual union is clearly one of the meanings to be associated with it. The man and the woman are 'one flesh' for another reason: 'the LORD God made a woman (*issa*) from the rib he had taken out of the man (*is*)' (Gen. 2.22). The man recognizes her:

> 'This is now bone of my bones
> and flesh of my flesh;
> she shall be called "woman",
> for she was taken out of man.' (Gen. 2.23)

The Hebrew word *issa* means both 'woman' and 'wife'. The first human pair is regarded as married. Marriage is the state of affairs in which becoming one flesh is divinely intended and authorized.

Two complementary sexes?

In the last 40 years or so, Anglicans and Roman Catholics have found something else in these Genesis texts. They have borrowed from physics the idea of 'complementarity'[3] and persuaded themselves that it can help them to understand what God did in making two sexes. One of the five core beliefs that Anglicans have been told that they hold about 'God's intention for human sexual activity'[4] is 'that the division of humankind into two distinct but *complementary* sexes is not something accidental or evil but is, on the contrary, something good established by God himself when he first created the human race'.[5] A weak definition of complementarity is provided: 'By complementary [*sic*] what is meant is that the differences between men and women were intended for the mutual good of each.' Any challenge to the sloppy consensus that Christians have always understood humanity to be comprised of two sexes, male and female, is beaten off: 'The overwhelming consensus of the Christian tradition has been that the division of humanity into two sexes was an original and integral part of God's creative plan.'[6] Pope John Paul II frequently used this idea in relation to the sexes: 'Woman complements man, just as man complements woman: men and women are

> Anglicans and Roman Catholics have borrowed the idea of 'complementarity' and persuaded themselves that it can help them to understand what God did in making two sexes

complementary. Womanhood expresses the "human" as much as manhood does, but in a different and complementary way.'[7]

This is an extraordinary development in recent theology. There are several reasons why it is inadequate. First, there are many people who do not identify themselves as either male or female. Susannah Cornwall has shown that the rigid distinction between male and female and the bad theology that supports it has further marginalized inter-sex and transgender or transsexual people.[8] Anthropologists sometimes speak of a 'third sex'.[9] Some Native American tribes contained *berdaches*, men and women, now called 'two-spirit' people, who adopted the gender roles associated with the sex that they were not. There are *hijras* in India and *guevedoce* in the Dominican Republic.[10] An Anglican collection of essays, designed to 'enable listening and dialogue' among warring Christians, commendably includes the testimony of a 'two-spirit' person who is also an Episcopalian priest in a covenanted relationship with a female partner.

> Some Native American tribes contained 'two-spirit' people, who adopted the gender roles associated with the sex that they were not

She explains how 'some Native (North) American cultures understand a multi-gendered system valuing gender diversity – male, female, male females, female males and non-specific genders and a balance of male and female known to some as "Two Spirit".'[11] Another Anglican work, designed to show how diffuse sexuality turns out to be in the corners of the earth to have been reached by the Anglican Communion, draws attention to *leiti* in Tonga, *kathoeys* in Thailand, 'ladyboys' in Brazil, and *fa'afafine* in Samoa.[12] These latter are 'men who identify themselves as women'.[13] The binary distinction between male and female is much more blurred than the modern story of complementarity purports to tell.

'Man': the one and only sex?

The second reason is that, until the eighteenth century, Western medicine did not believe that there were two sexes.[14] This is the oddest idea readers will find in this book, but it is very important to grasp. There was one sex, and it was called 'man'. 'Man' existed on a continuum between greater (male) and lesser (female) degrees of perfection. Everyone knows that Christianity used to talk about 'man'; it used to say that God was made 'man', and that 'We have sinned against you and against our *fellow men.*' This sexist language is still alive and well in many places (especially in Rome), and it provides the clearest evidence that for most of Christian history there were not two sexes but one ('man'), and women were included in it as inferior and imperfect versions of it. Bizarrely, language that used the male gender to include women ('he was made man' is a good example) used to be called *inclusive*, because Christians, like everyone else, thought men and women were included in the one sex. Only since the two-sex theory has taken root do we (rightly) think of such language as *ex*clusive.

> Until the eighteenth century, Western medicine did not believe that there were two sexes

In ancient biology men and women were thought to have the same reproductive equipment. The vagina was an inverted penis. The ovaries were 'really' testicles. The womb was 'really' a scrotum. The difference was whether these organs were internally or externally located. In Western medicine, based on the Greek physician and writer Galen (*c.*129–*c.*216 CE), women made sperm as well. (Why not? They had the means. They also had orgasms.) They became pregnant when their sperm and male sperm coagulated. The belief that women ejaculated sperm is found in the Second Testament:[15] 'Through faith also Sara herself received *strength to conceive seed*' (Heb. 11.11, KJV).[16]

(Aristotle had a different theory of conception. The man provided the 'form'; the woman provided the 'matter'. This theory influenced Aquinas and ultimately the Catholic tradition. But Galen's theory was prevalent in medical thought until the middle of the eighteenth century.)

Perfect men? Imperfect women?

Sexual difference lay in the degrees of perfection. Men's bodies were hotter and firmer, women's were cooler and softer. Classical historian Mathew Kuefler describes how the alleged hardness of men 'marked not only their moral austerity but also their role as sexual penetrators and sexual aggressors'.[17] Conversely, the 'softness of women denoted their role as sexually penetrated, and beyond that, the passive role they were expected to play not only in sexual relations but also in society generally'. Men in the Graeco-Roman world were thought to embody the positive qualities of 'physical and political strength, rationality, spirituality, superiority, activity, dryness, and penetration'. Women were thought to embody the negative qualities of 'physical and political weakness, irrationality, fleshliness, inferiority, passivity, wetness, and being penetrated'.[18] There *was* a strong sense of difference between men and women in the classical world but it was based on a sliding scale of being, not on two different sexes.

> The sense of difference between men and women in the classical world was based on a sliding scale of being, not on two different sexes

Good theology or bad ideology?

Once the ancient background is understood, the attitude of Jesus to women is seen to be remarkably counter-cultural. The old one-sex theory allowed for a felt commonality between men and women which the modern two-sex orthodoxy has weakened. Modernity has discovered and drawn attention to real biological differences, but has also greatly overemphasized their importance. Before we leave the one-sex theory it is important to note that this pre-modern view of sex was blind to the modern idea of equality. Within the human species, difference was allocated on grounds of alleged biological and social superiority. Some of the demeaning assumptions about women have already been noted. Given the (notorious) assumption that men are more perfect than women, it makes sense to argue that only men can represent God, or that God could become incarnate only in a man. How could God choose to be embodied in a creature that was self-evidently imperfect? But, since for us these assumptions are little more than demeaning and baseless, we cannot and should not allow them to continue to taint our theology.

> How could God choose to be embodied in a creature that was self-evidently imperfect?

There are other reasons for dismissing complementarity as a modern fantasy (which will be dealt with more briefly). Third, it is not just inter-sex and transgender people who are not straightforwardly going to find fulfilment in the 'opposite' sex. The solace of heterosexual coupledom (whether married or not) is denied to celibates and homosexuals, not to mention single people and widow(er)s. It is strange that a Church that over-values celibacy should start to advocate complementarity as well. Celibates don't need opposite-sex partners. Fourth, there is a logical contradiction about complementarity. Pope John Paul II wrestled with this. He argued that while man and woman are 'complete' in themselves, 'for forming a couple they are incomplete'.[19] But Todd Salzman and Michael Lawler rightly ask 'where the incompleteness and the need for complementarity are to be found in an individual that is complete in himself or herself, but is incomplete for forming a couple'.[20]

Finally, the mainstream churches have other, almost underhand reasons, for their doctrine of complementarity and their attempts to find this in Genesis and to pretend that Christian faith has possessed this doctrine in 'a seamless line from the world of Genesis to the early twenty-first century'.[21] Catholics can pretend to affirm the equality of men and women while denying women access to the priesthood. They are a different sex, the one that the incarnate Christ was not. Catholics and Protestants can pretend that homosexuality is wrong because when God made men and women, the creative purpose was for each to find fulfilment only in the other. Compulsory heterosexuality gets conveniently written into the creation script.

For many people, probably a clear majority, complementarity still rings true. That is because many women *do* seek special relationships with men, and men with women. Undoubtedly one of the meanings of sex is reproduction, and Christians are right to think that the Creator has arranged things so that men and women will seek each other out to form long-term partnerships and to have children. The error, and it is a pernicious one, is to suppose that just because it is 'natural' for a majority of one sex to seek union with the other, it is 'unnatural' for minorities of men and women, who have little or no interest in doing what the majority do, to seek to explore and pursue different desires. Others, as we have noted earlier, will not find that the modern binary sex divide coincides with their experience at all. The error is compounded by two further moves. The first is to *compel*, by law or social sanction, conformity to the majority view; the second is to claim that God's will, or God's plan, or the natural or created order, excludes deviation from the narrow norm absolutely. That doesn't sound like good news for minorities.

Different genders? Different roles?

Gender, gendering, gendered

Gender has many definitions.[22] Perhaps the most basic is 'the relations between women and men'.[23] Gender is pervasive. Harriet Bradley reminds us that 'all the institutions which make up our society (marriage, families, schools, workplaces, clubs, pubs, political organizations) are themselves *gendered* and are locations in which the *gendering* of individuals and relationships takes place'.[24] Churches, of course, are social institutions, and whenever they exclude or relegate women, they *proclaim* what they think of them and nurture others into taking these beliefs for granted.

There is a big divide between liberals and conservatives about gender, which often takes the form of an argument between 'essentialism' and 'constructionism'. In theological discussions about gender, essentialism is taken to be 'the doctrine that God created humanity into distinct sexes. Each is made for the other. Our created nature is to be male or female. Our natures cannot change.' Constructionism is the view that 'nothing about gender is fixed; everything is *constructed*'. It is the name given 'to theories that assume that relations of gender are neither revealed by God nor read off nature, but are historical constructions which are produced by societies and social groups'.[25] Extreme versions of the constructionist hypothesis should be avoided, since they imply that the human body is passively 'written upon' by society, offering little chance of individual resistance; or conversely that the individual is free to construct his or her self or personhood beyond the limits of the natural or divine order. If essentialism is limited to the view that humanity is created as God essentially intended, but with all the privations, distortions and estrangements that are the consequences of social and individual sinfulness, it need not invite objection.

The erosion of sexual 'dimorphism'

It is very clear that women have made enormous progress in education, in employment, in membership of male cartels and professions, and so on. A warship in the British Royal Navy will soon sail out of my home city of Plymouth, captained by a woman. Whether a job or a role is carried out by a woman or a man has become *a matter of indifference.* What *does* matter is that the person appointed is the best person available when every effort has been made to identify that person impartially. There has been 'an erosion of sexual dimorphism'[26] ('the assumption of two forms') in modern thought and practice. The problem for many conservatives in Judaism, Christianity and Islam is that the progress of women is thought to be contrary to 'the divinely revealed foundation of human sexuality found in scriptures', and brought about not by the movement of the Spirit in elevating women to their full human potential but by 'human infidelity to the divine will'. Many women, but by no means all, observes Christine Gudorf,

> have become competent and self-confident managers and leaders who share authority and decision making with others every day. They cannot become different people in their spiritual or domestic lives so as to be capable of rendering obedience, humility, or the self-effacement that religious traditions have deemed necessary modesty in women. All over the world educated, professional women come to expect that same affirmation in their domestic lives that they receive in their work lives: to be partners of their husbands, not subordinates (Eph.5:22–24, Quran 4:38); to be consulted and involved in joint decision making, not called to obedience.[27]

Of course 'all over the world' many millions of women enjoy none of the benefits Gudorf describes, and the amelioration of their plight remains a principal driving force for a renewed and vigorous feminist theology.[28] For most women in the Global North the situation is much as Gudorf says. She neatly observes that our basic moral obligations to the environment, to the poor, and to building a more just society, involve everyone, not just men; and just as women have

Making sense of sexual difference

become full members of society with a full share in its obligations, they seek to become full members of their religious communities too. The arguments frustrating these goals appear increasingly hollow whether advanced by popes, pastors or other patriarchs. A liberal understanding of gender is likely to rejoice in the full membership of women everywhere (as we shall shortly see, it is the fulfilment of a basic Christian hope). It does not follow that men should seek to do everything women can do, and conversely. What matters is that within and between the sexes men and women do what they are best suited to do. We can rejoice in our sexed bodies, and not seek to overcome them. Since it is true that men are generally stronger than women, it makes sense that they use their greater physical strength. Since women's bodies are better equipped for bonding with and nurturing children, it is better for those women who want to have children to have a greater share in at least the early months and years of childhood.

Celebrating difference in Christ

'Celebrating difference in Christ' may not quite be what the Church has traditionally done! However, there are theological grounds for thinking that difference may be celebrated, or, more precisely, for thinking that difference is an *aid* to communion among Christians because its propensity for arousing suspicion, exclusion, prejudice and violence has been overcome once and for all through what God accomplished and is accomplishing in Christ. 'Celebrating difference', then, is no vacuous political slogan that *pretends* that troubling differences of class, race, sex, gender and religion are not troubling after all. Still less should Liberal Theology be seen to be conniving with attempts to avoid painful conversations or (as

> When the otherness of the other is able to evoke wonder and acceptance, the destructive power of difference is overcome

our opponents often charge) borrowing the superficial language of a post-Christian culture that has lost its way. No, there are solid theological reasons for rejoicing in difference. When the otherness of the other is able to evoke wonder and acceptance, the destructive power of difference is overcome. Indifference, the cessation of violence, is installed instead.

Different sexes: one body

Speaking about two sexes requires biology. In a provocatively titled article, 'There is No Sexual Difference', Graham Ward remarks, 'The sexual in sexual difference is fundamentally physiological – it is that which can be read off bodies.'[29] Quite. But this starting point is queried. 'Why is difference theologically significant?' Why is biological difference important? One answer to the first question might be, to avoid female infanticide or 'gendercide', but even that painful answer has nothing to do with sexual difference as such. It draws attention to an appalling worldwide patriarchal crime against female bodies. There is no reason in physiology why a person lacking a penis should thereby lack respect or entitlement to a full life.

In the previous chapter the body was described as a 'field of communication', and the bodies of Christians were located within the mystical and eucharistic Body of Christ. It was suggested that membership of the Body of Christ can shape what believers do with their bodies, who they share them with, and how they contribute to the holiness of that body. In the context of thinking about sexual difference we now return to the Body of Christ and consider both its *composition* and its *mission*.

The queer Body of Christ

The Letter to the Ephesians contains a lengthy reflection on the then emerging Christian theology of marriage, but we will concentrate on how the author uses the symbol 'body of Christ' (Eph. 5.21–33). The relation between husband and wife is the (analogical) basis for the relation between Christ and the Church. Christ is the Bridegroom, and the Church is the Bride. The Church is also Christ's Body. Christ's Body, then, is clearly *female*. In Ephesians 5, we are not at a gay wedding. Christ, however, in his incarnate life had a human, *male* body. Christ and the Church also become a single body. ('He who loves his wife loves himself' – Eph. 5.28) That body is

> Christ and the Church also become a single body. That body is *both male and female*

both male and female. In other words, the Body of Christ is *androgynous*. Elsewhere (for example, 1 Cor. 12.12–31) the body is clearly androgynous. 'Christ is like a single body with its many limbs and organs' (1 Cor. 12.12, REB); 'Now you are Christ's body, and each of you a limb or organ of it' (1 Cor. 12.27, REB).

We may be able to notice features of this body, the Body of Christ, which escaped notice when the Second Testament was written. It is composed of male and female parts. It is a queer body. The point is not that all the parts are equal. Paul clearly recognized that some parts were more frail, dispensable and immodest than others. The point is that within the androgynous Body of Christ, *sexual* difference makes no difference. 'For we were all baptised by one Spirit into one body – whether Jews or Gentiles, slave or free – and we were all given the one Spirit to drink' (1 Cor. 12.13). (The baptismal formula quoted here appears to be the same quoted in Galatians 3.28, but here the tantalizing reference to male and female has been removed.) There are, of course, several other passages (especially in 1 Corinthians 11) where sexual difference *does* make a difference. Those passages are not overlooked in the present argument, but are located within the current Jewish theology of the time, while other latent elements of Paul's thought (here the composition of Christ's Body) are instead drawn out.

Next, it should be obvious that the incarnate Christ, the 'Lord' (in Latin, *dominus*), did not 'lord it over' (Mark 10.42) his disciples. His teaching and his life lived out in service to other people and for the sake of God's Reign is the antithesis of the swashbuckling Roman model of masculinity, based on aggressive, gendered power. Classicist Colleen Conway confirms, 'From the perspective of masculine identity in the ancient world, the implication of such teaching is that to be a disciple of Jesus means *to give up any claim to masculine status*'.[30] Christians

> Within the Body of Christ relations based on the dominance–submission model have no place whatever

perhaps need to rediscover that within the Body of Christ relations based on the dominance–submission model have no place whatever (and are best confined to bondage pornography where they are exposed for the evil they are).

Different Persons: one in being

Gender differences are best understood by another difference, of supreme importance to believers: the difference *within God*, between the divine Persons. Miroslav Volf has recently pointed out maleness and femaleness are features that we share with other *creatures*, and not with God, since God is not a creature. Handling differences, especially gender differences, between human persons is aided by a sharing in the differences between the *divine* Persons. This is a fine contribution that Theology can make to the discussion of gender: 'Instead of setting up ideals of femininity and masculinity, *we should root each in the sexed body and let the social construction of gender play itself out guided by the vision of the identity of and relations between divine persons.*'[31]

Gendered relations are distorted everywhere, and their distortion is subject to local variation. The contribution of Christians to the healing of these relations is to begin with these differences and to seek to transform them so that they resemble more the differences that are found in God, where Persons are equal, derive their being from each other, and are one in Love. 'We must both affirm equality between men and women and seek to change social practices in which the inferiority of women is embodied and through which it is perpetuated.'[32] In the mystery of the Trinity, difference is not allowed to become distorted by allowing silly patterns of dominance and submission to ruin the Communion that God is.

Different genders: one humanity

St Paul had a remarkable vision for a renewed humanity by means of the death and resurrection of Christ. He wrote: 'There is neither Jew nor Greek, neither slave nor free, nor is there male and female, for you are all one in Christ Jesus' (Gal. 3.28). Unfortunately that verse has nearly always been heavily qualified by other Second Testament passages where gender difference is assumed and applied. The literature on this verse is vast. Susannah Cornwall has drawn attention to the form of the couplets,

> 'neither Jew *nor* Greek,
> neither slave *nor* free,
> neither male *and* female'.

Making sense of sexual difference

The couplet 'male *and* female' is joined by a *con*junction ('and'): the other two are joined by a *dis*junction ('neither ... nor'). She suggests the inclusive 'male and female' is the single 'male-and-female' as a 'socially-limiting construct'[33] that passes away in Christ. This idea is highly congruent with the one sex existing in a single continuum discussed earlier. In the new creation, 'biology is not to be the primary or most defining thing about members of the new community'. The Christian community anticipates in its restored relations the new, perfected humanity as Christ has redeemed it. 'The end – the cessation – of male-and-female is the end – the *telos* – of humanity.'[34] Or, in the terms I have used in this chapter, sexual difference becomes a matter of indifference. Restored relations at the end of time will cover more than just the uneasy relations between the sexes. Ethnicity and class are also named in this famous verse. Whether sexual *orientation* can ever be a matter of indifference is the subject of the next chapter.

5

Making sense of homosexuality – from disgust to delight

Much has been written on the question whether lesbian and gay people in the Church can be partnered, married, ordained or become bishops. I confess to adding to the pile.[1] In this chapter, something different will be tried. First, summaries of very recent versions of 'traditionalist' and 'liberal' arguments about same-sex relationships and the nature of marriage are set out in the form of objections and counter-claims. Second, each of these is then analysed. Readers will not be surprised to find that the traditionalist case is found to be theologically wanting, and a pastoral disaster. Third, the argument is broadened out by further consideration of ancient gender theory (which was opened up in Chapter 4). These new considerations will be shown to add weight to the liberal case. Can Christian marriage be offered to same-sex partners? That question will be discussed in Chapter 6, after getting to the bottom of what marriage is.

In December 2011 a very full edition of the journal *Anglican Theological Review* was devoted to the topic of same-sex relationships and the nature of marriage.[2] Two groups of theologians, one traditionalist (four men) and one liberal (two men, two women), each presented their case and then responded to their opponents' case. Several other theologians then commented on the exchanges. We will now look at the arguments.

Arguments about same-sex marriage: a recent 'dialogue'

The traditionalists' case: compulsory heterosexuality

A clear, but quite lengthy, case for the traditional theological position about homosexuality was put by the traditionalist team. I have tried to summarize their case as fairly as I can in ten objections, listed below.

1. Liberals wrongly seek 'a redefinition of the institution of marriage itself' which is unacceptable to the great majority of Christians and churches.³ Biblical marriage is exclusively between a man and a woman.⁴ Marriage is defined as a permanent arrangement between a man and a woman. This might be called *the definitional objection*.

   > 'Biblical marriage is exclusively between a man and a woman'

2. Liberals flout 'the clear opposition of Scripture'⁵ to homosexuality and to the blessing of same-sex unions. This is *the biblical objection*.
3. Liberals have a 'general tendency to water down the basis and nature of Christian attitudes and way of life'.⁶ The inspiration of liberals 'will have come more from assimilation to modern culture than from following Jesus in learning how better to understand and live by the Scriptures.'⁷ This is *the cultural objection*.
4. Liberals refuse to acknowledge that God has designed 'a lifelong exclusive heterosexual relationship as the proper context for bringing up children'.⁸ This is *the essentialist* or *heterosexual objection*.
5. Liberal accounts of marriage are deficient because they ignore the 'connection of marriage, in God's plan, to the fruitfulness of humanity through the creation of children and families'.⁹ This is *the procreative objection*.
6. Liberals don't acknowledge that, even after God has restored the order of creation so that it shares in the resurrection of Christ, that order will remain heterosexual. The 'continuity of the created order includes human nature as created by God'. The 'divine intention' has been declared once and for all in 'the union of male and female in one flesh'.¹⁰ This is *the eschatological objection*.
7. The liberal case is mired in the destructive attempt of science and technology to bend nature to its will. Liberals compromise with the 'shift in Western thought from a discernment of meaning and purpose in nature to the attitude that nature – including our

own human nature – is something on which we are free to impose our own will and purposes'.[11] This is *the technocratic objection*.
8. Liberals ignore natural law and the 'objective moral order'. Heterosexual marriage and its procreative purpose can both be read off the natural, moral order, even without the benefit of the Christian revelation.[12] This is *the natural law objection*.
9. Liberals turn scientific accounts of homosexuality to their own purposes. There is insufficient evidence at present to conclude that 'same-sex attraction is *innate*',[13] or 'natural'. This is *the evidential deficiency objection*.
10. Liberals should not presume that homosexual orientation cannot be changed. 'There is still evidence that some positive and beneficial change can and does take place as a result of some ministries and programs.'[14] All Christians have to learn that 'to refuse to indulge sexual urges is part of the general spiritual discipline that needs to be developed in many other areas of life and is part of the way of the cross'.[15] No exemption for gays here, then. This is *the spiritual deficiency objection*.

The liberals' case: 'apposite' not 'opposite' sexes

The liberal team presents a case that does not defer to the conservatives, or to their frame of reference. Here is a short summary of their views.

1. Marriage is about *holiness*. The Church 'should marry same-sex couples because it requires their testimony to the love of Christ and the Church, and because it recognizes that same-sex couples stand in need of sanctification no less than opposite-sex couples do.'[16] Marriage is 'an ascetic discipline'.[17] 'Same-sex couples must avoid unchastity: they must marry.'[18] This is *the holiness claim*.

   > Same-sex couples *stand in need of sanctification* no less than opposite-sex couples do

2. The Holy Spirit is thought to be active in the churches where there is recognition of the holiness of partnered same-sex couples.[19] A (by now familiar) analogy is drawn between the situation facing the early Church at the time of the conversion of the Gentiles, and our own time, described in Acts 10—15. 'The circumcised believers who had come with Peter were astonished that the gift

of the Holy Spirit had been poured out even on the Gentiles' (Acts 10.45). Peter had asked 'Can any man forbid water, that these should not be baptized, which have received the Holy Ghost as well as we?' (Acts 10.47, KJV). Paraphrasing Peter's question, the liberals ask, regarding same-sex couples, 'Can anyone withhold the rite for blessing these couples who "have received the Holy Spirit just as we have" (Acts 10.47)?'[20] This is *the divine intervention claim*.

3 The procreative purpose of marriage is not absolute, so the heterosexual requirement is not necessary. Now that the Messiah has come, it is *spiritual* or 'qualitative' fruitfulness that is required.[21] That was why the argument for celibacy in the early Church was so powerful. This is *the general fruitfulness claim*.

4 Liberals are faithful to the Gospel and to the 'Mission of God' in seeking to engage lesbian and gay couples and to offer them marriage.[22] This is *the evangelistic claim*.

5 Liberals (in their response to the traditionalist paper) make a whole new point about what they do with the Bible. They are addressing directly the very people for whom the biblical writers had no time:

> We also read with an expanded community of readers, including many whom the church has not previously recognized and some whom the biblical texts do not address as subjects. In the authorial perspective of some biblical texts, women, wives, slaves, Gentiles, and sexual minorities are subordinated as persons and silenced as mutual interpreters of God's revelation. The expanded readership of the Christian church now questions these attitudes and the social presuppositions on which they were based. We read scriptural texts about marriage in a culture and world of ideas where the model of the authority of husband over wife, master over slave, and parent over child has been substantially revised in the direction of egalitarianism, mutuality, and democracy. We welcome this development as positive and related to Christian social witness.[23]

This is *the hermeneutical claim*.

6 The liberals redefine orientation in terms of how Jesus Christ transforms it. They ask,

> What is a sexual orientation? It is an orientation of desire. Since Christ satisfies 'the desires of every living thing' (Psalm 145.16), a

sexual orientation, theologically speaking, must be this: a more or less settled tendency by which Christ orients desire toward himself, through the desire for another human being.

> A sexually oriented person develops and is morally improved through a relationship with someone of the *apposite* sex, typically but not necessarily the *opposite* sex

This redefinition allows them to speak of a person becoming married to another, not of the *opposite*, but the *apposite*, sex: 'A sexually oriented person is someone who develops and is morally improved through a relationship with someone of the *apposite* sex, typically but not necessarily the *opposite* sex.' This is *the transformational claim*.

Examining the arguments

The liberals' case: a disappointment

While I have no quarrel with the liberal case, I think it was largely ineffective, and it is easy to see how it was to make little headway against the apparent certainties of the conservative position.[24] Marriage *has* always been between a woman and a man. The change the liberals want *is* a momentous one. It might have been better to have drawn attention to changes that have already occurred since biblical times, both with regard to marriage and to various other sexual practices. Mark Jordan reminds the conservatives that there are plenty of sexual practices that Christian teaching has always condemned but which are 'now considered perfectly acceptable – along with denigrations of marriage, elaborate codes of purity and pollution, and lurid depictions of the demonic dangers posed by women'.[25] Genital activities, he reminds us, now commonplace in marriage, used to be regarded as 'unnatural and even sodomitic'. 'To pluck out one topic of condemnation while ignoring all those around it is the worst sort of proof-texting.'

With regard to marriage, the changes since biblical times have been momentous. Biblical marriage assumed the gendered view of women discussed in Chapter 4. We have grown out of silly phallic doctrines of male headship, the necessity of female obedience, the out-playing of dominance and submission, and all the other apparatuses of patriarchy.

Making sense of homosexuality

Marriage is more than ever a partnership of equals, characterized by mutuality and reciprocity. Marriage has turned out to have been a remarkably flexible institution (even for many Christians accommodating divorce and further marriages). The admission of same-sex partners to marriage would be a continuation of the changes that have already been negotiated. The argument for change needs to be provided *along with* the theology that supports it (Chapter 6), and this was not done.

There were other weaknesses in the liberal case. The analogy between the admission of Gentiles to the sacrament of baptism and the admission of lesbian and gay couples to the sacrament of marriage, however much it resonates among those for whom the analogy works, is always going to be what it is – an *analogy* – and it doesn't take too much expertise to point out the obvious lack of comparison (the '*dis*analogies') between the two cases. Some of the uses of Scripture are certain to be found implausible. 'Orientation' cannot be so simply redefined by reference to a verse of a psalm and then given a new Christological sense. The liberal side seem as guilty as their opponents in conscripting texts to support prior positions.

A careful reader might note how *similar* the opposing positions actually are. One would expect Christians to have lots of common ground. Yet both sides have little trouble in believing themselves to have arrived at right interpretations of biblical texts, however traditional or innovative their conclusions are. Both sides talk about 'homosexuality' as if it was something the biblical writers knew about. Yet the term, and the new assumptions that went with it, was coined only in 1869.[26] Men undoubtedly had sex with men in ancient times, as the Levitical code acknowledges (and forbids), and Paul condemns it too. But neither side acknowledges the reasons why men having sex with men in the Bible is thought to be wrong. (We will return to this important consideration in the next section.)

> Neither side acknowledges the reasons why men having sex with men in the Bible is thought to be wrong

The traditionalists' case: a disgrace

Since the points made by the traditionalists crop up continually in pulpits and church documents, it is important to show that the liberals are able to respond robustly to each of them. It is true that biblical marriage is exclusively between a man and a woman (point 1). But biblical marriage is also patriarchal and hierarchical (where it is encouraged at all). The traditionalists need to say why they are able to depart conveniently from biblical teaching about the patriarchal form of marriage (and, of course, about the requirement of no-divorce) yet remain stubbornly committed to one particular feature of it (that it can only happen between a man and a woman).

The assumption that there is a 'clear opposition of Scripture' to homosexuality (point 2) is a blithe assertion, repeated by official documents and conferences until it has become almost a mantra. The holiness code of Leviticus condemns men having sex with men (Lev. 18.22; 20.13), but it also condemns men having sex with menstruating women (Lev. 19.24), and allows men to have sex with slaves, provided they own them (Lev. 19.20–22). Christians obey Christ, not an old law based on purity and property, necessary though it may once have been. Why do the traditionalists assert that Christians must obey just *these* commandments?

The sin of the men of Sodom was a failure of hospitality.[27] That is the clear meaning of Jesus' references to the city (Matt. 10.15; Luke 10.12). All the other proof-texts are at best shaky. Women having unnatural sexual relations (Rom. 1.26) need not refer to what we call lesbianism. It could just as easily refer to women having oral or anal sex with men, as Clement of Alexandria and Augustine both thought.[28] The traditionalists assume that the people referred to in 1 Corinthians 6.9–11 and 1 Timothy 1.10 are 'those who practise homosexual behaviour',[29] yet this is easily (and convincingly) disputed.[30] The point is not that the traditionalists are wrong, but that their interpretations and assumptions are problematic and by no means justify the confidence they have in them.

> The point is not that the traditionalists are wrong, but that their interpretations and assumptions are problematic and by no means justify the confidence they have in them

Other points can be dismissed more briefly. Why are liberals singled out as diluting the faith and assimilating it to modern culture (point 3)? That is what Catholics think that Evangelicals do. Liberals engage with modern culture, and try to offer the gospel so that it actually sounds like good news. Liberals don't have a problem with God designing families so that children have a mother and a father (point 4). The issue of adoption is a separate one. Liberals acknowledge that marriages should be fruitful (point 5). They question whether marital fruitfulness must always mean having children. Many infertile couples, and fertile couples choosing to remain infertile ('chosen childlessness') are admitted to the sacrament of marriage with no fuss or questions asked. The Church has never insisted on biological fertility as a condition for admission to marriage.

Is heterosexuality written into the created *and* the restored order of the world (point 6)? That seems a very dubious claim for traditionalists to make, at least on the basis of Scripture. It is possible that they have not read their Bibles thoroughly enough. The point of Jesus' remark that in the resurrection couples will be 'like the angels' (Luke 20.36) is that in eternity sexual differences are brought to an end. Liberals have probably been more active than traditionalists in opposing the dominance of nature by technology (point 8). Gay people don't impose their will and purposes on nature. Yes, they constitute a sexual *minority*, but where does the expectation that everyone should be straight come from? Nature herself is more diverse, less 'di-morphic' than the traditionalists envisage (point 8). The charge that liberals manipulate the scientific evidence (point 9) is remarkable, and overlooks the traditionalists' own 'tendentious choice of scientific authorities on questions of sexuality'.[31]

The traditionalists hang on to the notion that in some cases a change of orientation is possible (point 10). Leaving aside the presumption that homosexuality is a sickness requiring treatment, they should read the testimony of the evangelical Christian Jeremy Marks, a man so committed to the 'ex-gay ideal' of coming out of homosexuality that he founded Courage,[32] to minister to gay Christians seeking to overcome their affliction. After 12 years he, in his own words, 'startled the evangelical world by publicly repudiating the ex-gay movement, proclaiming that it did more harm than good'.[33] The liberals claim that 'scientific evidence about changing orientations is unanimous'. They note that the American Psychiatric Association removed homosexual orientation from its list of diseases in 1973 and that the American Psychological Association declared 'reparative therapy' *unethical* in 1979. 'Whatever the mechanics of causation', they say,

> health care professionals acknowledge sexual orientation as a given, prior to choice, a natural aptitude. It may be socially shaped but it does not go away. Minority orientations, whether they number in the few or many millions, cannot be ethically coerced into majority patterns of relationship.[34]

Pastoral wretchedness

The traditionalists' case is responsible for much pastoral wretchedness. It directly creates intense distress. It still pushes people into unsuitable marriages. The liberals justifiably retort,

> The trouble with marrying people to members of the opposite sex, when the opposite sex is not apposite for them, is that it undermines marriage. It leads to lying of the body, adultery, and divorce, instead of the truthfulness of the body, faithfulness, and constancy.[35]

The complete package of conservative teaching about homosexuality is ghastly. It undermines the best of Anglican pastoral teaching which begins with the attempt to understand pastoral need and pain. It underscores the persecution of sexual minorities and homophobic violence all over the world. It damages the faith in the eyes of non-Christians who understand the traditional case as a failure of love, a failure of justice, and a tragic spiritual blindness. It confuses the necessity of genuine sacrifice for Christ's sake with the unnecessary pain caused by homophobic intolerance. It trivializes the real suffering it inflicts on Christian people, who seek to follow the One who says to them:

> 'Come to me, all you who are weary and burdened, and I will give you rest. Take my yoke upon you and learn from me, for I am gentle and humble in heart, and you will find rest for your souls. For my yoke is easy and my burden is light.' (Matt. 11.28–30)

There is no recognition of the long tradition of Bible misuse in which the traditionalists now stand. Similar uses of the Bible have endorsed anti-Semitism, the judicial murder of thousands of witches, the endorsement of racism, of slavery, of sexism, and so on.[36] Learned theologians and church leaders all over the world have managed once again to distance themselves from the horrendous consequences of their teaching while convincing themselves of their moral rectitude and of their position on the highest of high moral and theological ground.

Gender again

As arguments continue to rage, there may actually be *new* ground that is capable of further influencing the outcome. In the previous chapter, the notion of complementarity was critiqued, and the ancient view was stated that until the eighteenth century there was only one sex: 'man'. Women were less perfect specimens of the same, single sex. The term 'spectrum' has been well chosen to express the range of sexualities covered by the theory. Diana Swancutt, a strong advocate of the one-sex theory, explains:

> ancients did not conceive of the people assigned to the ends of the spectrum as referring to two genetically differentiated sexes, male, and female. Rather, ancients constructed the human physique on a one-body, multigendered model with the perfect body deemed 'male/man'.[37]

This view, which helps to explain the background to historical discrimination against women, also helps to explain why men having sex with men is condemned in the Bible. Since this view is no longer held, it cannot provide the foundation for any objections to homosexuality. It just falls away. How, exactly, are gender and homosexuality connected?

One answer is *feminization*. When a man has anal sex with another man, one of them lets himself be penetrated. He lets himself become as a woman, and that was regarded as a perilous thing to allow. There seems to be broad agreement in the classical world about this, and it is found in the First Testament too. 'If a man lies with a man as one does with a woman, both of them have done what is detestable. They must be put to death; their blood will be on their own heads' (Lev. 20.13; 18.22). But we now know why men having anal sex with men is a capital offence in the Levitical code.[38] It is not because there was something Anglicans call 'homosexual practice' going on that God doesn't like. If you are penetrated ('as one does with a woman') you are feminized. You abandon your masculinity. Since it is so much better and more perfect to be a man than to be a woman, you are crazy to compromise your masculinity! Paul believed that a man reflected the image and glory of God, while a woman was a lesser reflection of God's image and glory, possessing it insofar as she resembled a man (1 Cor. 11.7). The one-sex theory explains this. The nearer an individual is to the male end of the spectrum, the more likely he is to image God. Any male behaviour which appeared to be feminine undermined a man's masculinity completely.

> Any male behaviour which appeared to be feminine undermined a man's masculinity completely

The disease of effemination

Another answer, which also has to do with the 'gender spectrum', was the fear of sliding down it. It was also a gradient – 'the gender gradient'[39] – down which men could readily slide. There was a slippery slope to be avoided, from masculinity, through effeminacy, to femininity. Swancutt calls this fear 'the disease of effemination'.[40] Men were haunted by the question, 'If women were not different in kind, but simply a lesser, incomplete version of men, what was there to keep men from sliding down the axis into the female realm?'[41] Manhood involved constant recognition in public and private behaviour, since it was 'not a state to be definitely achieved but something always under construction and constantly open to scrutiny'.[42]

A good case can be made for claiming that the 'disease of effemination' is the theological problem lying behind Paul's chastisement of the Gentiles having unnatural sex in Romans 1.18–32. Almost no biblical passage has been the subject of so much attention (and one can despair of arriving at a conclusion with any confidence).[43] The price to be paid for a man who failed to achieve self-mastery and/or who succumbed to taking the passive role in sex was to traverse the gender continuum and destroy his 'hard-won maleness'.[44] On this view, if a man consents to be penetrated he forsakes an important part of the God-likeness in him. He wilfully allows his own body to be treated as if it were the body of a woman. The mysterious link between passive male sex and idolatry now becomes explicable. A man abandons his God-likeness if he is buggered by another man. His giving in to shameful lusts threatens the very characteristic of masculinity that males share with the divine.

> Giving in to shameful lusts threatens the very characteristic of masculinity that males share with the divine

Liberal confidence in same-sex love

Liberals do not have a problem with same-sex love. Derrick Sherwin Bailey's *Homosexuality and the Western Christian Tradition* (1955),[45] H. Kimball-Jones' *Towards a Christian Understanding of the Homosexual* (1967),[46] and Norman Pittenger's *Time for Consent* (1970)[47] are notable, liberal, ground-breaking books that bring theological understanding and Christian charity to a persecuted and often despised minority. Occasionally new arguments arise that can add weight to the original work done by liberal theologians. Classical scholars have heightened our understanding of gender in the ancient world, and against this background, the proscription of same-sex love and the reasons for its being declared sinful are seen to make good sense. It is a pity that the liberal team in the *Anglican Theological Review* did not pay more attention to the historical relativism of conservative arguments, and expose them for their failure to uncover both the ancient roots of gender prejudice and the modern roots of terms like 'homosexuality' and 'heterosexuality' which they find in Scripture almost without looking. Once attention is given to some of the ideas of the last two chapters, like the one-sex, male–female continuum, the danger of effemination, or the compromise of the male image of the male God by men doing un-masculine things (like being penetrated), some of the reasons why same-sex sex was feared and hated at last come to light. Once the surrounding context of the biblical prohibitions is allowed to assist in explaining what they say, they can be seen to be based on gendered assumptions that no longer have any point or moral force.

We no longer think that it is better to be a man than a woman. Men still enjoy enormous social advantages over women in many societies, but there is nothing intrinsically or essentially inferior about being a woman. Yes, there are (to us) obvious differences in the genitalia of men and women, apart from their internal and external locations. The discovery of these differences led to a shocking conclusion: there are (at least) two biological sexes! It makes good sense to speak of two sexes, but there is no doubt that this modern way of speaking has several disadvantages. It overemphasizes biological difference and contributes to a sense of cultural warfare between the sexes. It gives rise to unhelpful notions of the complementarity of the sexes. It creates a 'dimorphism' that leaves no room for countless people who do not find that they rest easily in rigid categories of 'male' and 'female' that have been created for them, or whose desires do not accord with the pattern that is supposed to determine them.

These disadvantages do not add up to a plea to reinstate the old male–female continuum. That would be impossible, and the social assumptions that were once built on supposed biological 'facts' like men's greater heat or women's weaker sperm, are nowadays dismissed with incredulity. But once the old continuum is banished, it is not just the supposed inferiority of women that falls away. The idea that there is something immoral about men being or behaving like women falls away as well. The fear of homosexuality remains gender based.

6

Making sense of marriage – from patriarchy to partnership

This chapter has three aims. First, it will commend several theological pictures of marriage, endorsing them all. These pictures are hugely important for anyone contemplating becoming married. Second, it will show that these pictures of marriage enable the churches to offer marriage to same-sex couples. Third, it will show how the admission of same-sex couples to marriage is fully consistent with the sources for Christian sexual ethics examined in Chapter 1.

Marriage as it is found in the Bible and Tradition is frankly unacceptable in the twenty-first century. Scripture and Tradition can still be read so as to actually *endorse* the type of marriage that women and egalitarian-minded men now find intolerable. Those millions of evangelical Christians who understand the Bible literally wherever possible condemn women to psychological subjugation to their husbands. In marriage husbands do the loving; wives do the submitting. Wives 'should submit to their husbands in everything' (Eph. 5.24). There are plenty more texts which, even as they fall from the mouths of male preachers, enforce an asymmetrical or unbalanced view of gender and of marriage that persists even in evangelical churches today throughout the world, and licenses nervous debates about whether the Bible teaches 'male headship'[1] (clearly it does), and if so what to do about it. I reluctantly agree with secular historians that, despite regular exceptions, the institution of marriage has licensed inordinate male power over women.[2] The good news is that there is nothing about marriage that requires it to be a patriarchal institution, and in the theological pictures that follow, it will be seen to be a deeply egalitarian one, grounded in the very being of the Triune God.

Seven pictures of marriage

We have already looked at two of the most important pictures – marriage as a 'communion of persons' and as a 'gift of bodies'.

A Communion of Persons

In Chapter 3 the idea that people are made in the image of God was commended by concentrating on the relations between human persons and building an analogy with the relations between the divine Persons within God. These Persons are distinct Persons, yet their individuality does not compromise the indivisible unity that God is. God's life is Communion. Human life is made for communion, too, yet it is marred by disruption and violence. It needs redemption. Everyone is made for communion with one another and with God. Marital status provides no prior condition, still less a guarantee, for the possibility of living in communion. That said, being married is a communion of persons that involves deep physical intimacy. It follows that love-making in marriage, together with the sharing of marital life which it expresses, provides a powerful and perhaps supreme instance of communion among or between persons. Yes, in this communion of persons, the divine Communion of Persons appears and lives.

A gift of bodies

A second picture of marriage, also viewed in Chapter 3, was painted in gorgeous eucharistic colours. Christ's giving of his body over to his followers was seen to be a startling evocation of what happens elsewhere, when a person gives and receives the body of his or her partner. Marriage, of course, is not necessary for the giving over of one's body in abandon to a beloved other. But Christians insist that there is something unique about marriage, that in the giving and receiving of persons, to and from each other, exclusively, faithfully and permanently, a new vista opens up upon marriage. The physical expression of love becomes intertwined with the sharing of lives in a deep commitment, which is unconditionally expressed by the self-giving of God for us in love and in death. That is why marriage is sometimes called a *mimesis*.[3] 'Mimesis' means a strong representation or imitation of something else ('mime' and 'mimic' come from the same root). Marriage mimes the love of Christ for the Church. The author of Ephesians would agree that marriage is mimesis. After quoting the verse from Genesis that a married couple 'become one flesh' (Gen. 2.24), he adds, 'This is a profound mystery – but I am talking about Christ and the church' (Eph. 5.32). The 'profound mystery' is that love within marriage takes on the character of something *divine* – Christ's own love for the Church.

> Marriage mimes the love of Christ for the Church

A covenant

An important document from the Second Vatican Council says: 'The intimate partnership of married life and love has been established by the Creator and qualified by His laws, and is rooted in the conjugal covenant of irrevocable personal consent.'[4] Marriage, apparently for the first time in Roman Catholic thought, is called a *foedus*, a covenant, 'an image and a sharing in the covenant of love between Christ and the Church'. John Calvin is the author of the idea of marriage as a covenant in Protestant traditions.[5] With careful qualification, God's relationship to God's people in the First Testament can be seen as a covenant.

Part of the contemporary value of speaking of marriage as a covenant is its implied contrast with contract.[6] The Jesuit theologian Paul Palmer made the point well, 40 years ago. While he doubtless exaggerated and polarized the differences between them, the contrasts he made are listed below in two columns.

The characteristics of contracts	The characteristics of covenants
are about things,	are about people,
engage the services of people,	engage persons,
can be broken;	cannot be broken without personal loss and broken hearts;
are secular,	are sacred,
best understood by lawyers,	appreciated better by poets and theologians,

| witnessed by people with the state as guarantor, have an economic value only. | witnessed by God with God as guarantor, require mental, emotional and spiritual maturity.[7] |

This understanding of marriage as a covenant, offered by the Church to marrying couples whether or not they are believers, expresses the specialness of their intentions in a way that also nudges them towards faith. Marriage offers a different level of human relationship, which contrasts with other personal relationships and is also a defence against the temptation within advanced societies to treat people as things by introducing notions of dominance, ownership, calculation, or obsolescence. Marriage requires, but cannot be exhausted by, the legal frameworks that specify it. Couples may long for a language that articulates the meanings of their commitments, in the first place to themselves and to each other, and covenant language provides it.

An image of the New Covenant

The covenant that is marriage tells us about what Christianity is, for the Christian faith is nothing else but a covenant: the New Covenant, or Testament. The New Covenant *is* Christianity. It is what Christ seals with his own blood (Matt. 26.28; Mark 14.24; 1 Cor. 11.25). It defines the arrangement of the Christian Scriptures into two parts. Pope John Paul II made the striking connection between the covenant of marriage and the covenant that is Christianity:

> The communion of love between God and people, a fundamental part of the Revelation and faith experience of Israel, finds a meaningful expression in the marriage covenant which is established between a man and a woman.
>
> For this reason the central word of Revelation, 'God loves His people,' is likewise proclaimed through the living and concrete word whereby a man and a woman express their conjugal love. Their bond of love becomes the image and the symbol of the covenant which unites God and His people.[8]

What the Pope envisages here is the mingling of divine love with human love such that the human love comes to fruition in the 'partnership of the whole of life' (a medieval definition of marriage). That

Making sense of marriage

partnership is already a sharing in the divine covenant with humankind, and Christ's covenant with all the people of God. The bond of love between married couples is what they have in common with the covenant-love of God for God's people. Use of the terms 'image' and 'symbol' provide the continuity between the two loves. Pastorally put, couples are able to find their way to God through the love they already have for one another.

> Couples are able to find their way to God through the love they already have for one another

A mutual ministry

There is a controversial detail of Western thought about the marital sacrament, that marriage is the only sacrament that does not, or rather did not, need to be administered by a priest. A couple is validly married (assuming no impediment) when they make vows to each other in the present tense before witnesses. The priest pronounces them married, and blesses them, but the blessing is not what makes the marriage (as it is in Eastern churches). The Council of Trent required the presence of a priest for the marriage to be valid, and both Catholics and Protestants reacted to the abuses of clandestine marriages by tightening their grip on the entry to marriage. But the presence of the priest or minister at a wedding should not eclipse the ancient understanding that the couple *minister the sacrament to each other*.

The great contemporary relevance of this detail lies in the couple being co-ministers. They are co-equal in their mutual ministry. They marry each other. Two further, simple points may be tellingly made about this. First, the joint ministry of the couple is a fine basis for equal regard and full mutuality over every detail of the marriage. The couple are full and equal partners in the common enterprise. There is no suggestion that one loves while the other obeys. Second, everything they do for one another is a ministry, an ad*ministeri*ng of their sacrament. One of the supplementary prayers in the *Common Worship* Marriage Service comes near to saying this when the priest asks God to

> Everything they do for one another is a ministry, an ad*ministeri*ng of their sacrament

Give them wisdom and devotion in ordering their common life,
that each may be to the other
a strength in need, a counsellor in perplexity,
a comfort in sorrow and a companion in joy.

A unity of heart, body and mind

Jesus himself spoke of marriage as 'one flesh'. He cites Genesis 2.24, where the term first occurs (Mark 10.8–9; Matt. 19.5–6), and immediately adds, 'Therefore what God has joined together, let man not separate.' Various meanings have been thought to flow from this uncompromising definition of marriage, most obviously that a marriage approved by God is indissoluble. In the Genesis story the man and the woman are 'one flesh' because the woman has been made from the flesh and bones of the man. The man recognizes his own body in the body of the woman that the Lord God brought to him (Gen. 2.22). The saying about 'one flesh' has not been favourable to women over time. It has been used to support the legal inclusion of a wife's body and property within her husband's body and property. She belonged to her husband in a total, irrevocable and unidirectional way.

The idea of union between husband and wife contributes to a very different atmosphere in the *Common Worship* Marriage Service of the Church of England (2000) where marriage is declared to be

> a gift of God in creation
> through which husband and wife may know the grace of God.
> It is given
> that as man and woman grow together in love and trust,
> they shall be *united with one another in heart, body and mind,*
> as Christ is united with his bride, the Church.
>
> The gift of marriage brings husband and wife together
> in the delight and tenderness of sexual union
> and joyful commitment to the end of their lives.
> It is given as the foundation of family life
> in which children are [born and] nurtured
> and in which each member of the family, in good times and in bad,
> may find strength, companionship and comfort,
> and grow to maturity in love.[9]

Making sense of marriage

This beautiful evocation of the purposes of marriage affirms 'the delight and tenderness' of sexual union. The tone contrasts starkly with that of the Book of Common Prayer, which warns that marriage 'is not by any to be enterprised, nor taken in hand, unadvisedly, lightly, or wantonly, to satisfy men's carnal lusts and appetites, like brute beasts that have no understanding'.[10] Here the 'one flesh' that a couple becomes is understood from a developmental perspective – what the couple can become. Their union is a 'holistic' one involving 'heart, body and mind'.

An anticipation of the end!

The joy of marriage anticipates the end of the world? Could anything sound crazier? Well, several parables and sayings of Jesus use images of marriage and wedding feasts. The triumph of God's purposes over all that opposes them is symbolized as a cosmic wedding reception. An angel tells St John, 'Write: "Blessed are those who are invited to the wedding supper of the Lamb!"' (Rev. 19.9; cf. 21.2, 9). The use of imagery drawn from marriage to express deeper truths about God is called 'nuptial mysticism'.

> The triumph of God's purposes over all that opposes them is symbolized as a cosmic wedding reception

Nuptial mysticism assists the churches' renewed engagement with marriage in a social climate indifferent to it. There has to be a very high premium placed on marriage in order for any kind of nuptial mysticism to work at all. Whatever the relationship between Christ and the Church, or between the Lamb and the Heavenly City, the symbols most honed to express it are derived from the experience of the marital union. The union of husband and wife in a common life becomes the material out of which the union of God with the estranged world is envisaged. Biblical marriage presupposes betrothal before marriage, the 'spousals' before the 'nuptials'.[11] The transition from one to the other involves a period of waiting and expectation, finally and joyfully expressed at the nuptial banquet. As the Church awaits the culmination of the ages and the restitution of all things through Christ (Acts 3.21), marital imagery lies at the base of the expression of this hope. Marital love is capable of imaging the divine love for the world that triumphs over everything that is set against it. Nuptial mysticism shows how wedding receptions can consciously carry rich theological significance, since the Bible itself uses them to prefigure the triumph of divine love at the end of time.

These core doctrinal themes provide a clear Christian framework for couples to experience inductively the divine love for them through the love they have for one another. Those responsible for the Church's teaching ministry need to understand that successful learning is likely to be grounded experientially, and the mutual love of partners for each other provides the inductive basis for discovery of that deeper, divine love that already embraces them. Just as the Christian doctrine of God shapes the Christian understanding of marriage, so the experience of marriage leads on to the experience of God whose love mingles with all human loves.

The doctrinal heart of marital theology is God, and nothing else but God, revealed in Incarnation, Trinity and Eucharist. That theology yields themes of mutuality and reciprocity; of hope in what is and is to come; of covenanted regard that exposes contractual convenience, of the giving and receiving of bodies, of growing commitment, love and faithfulness.

> The doctrinal heart of marital theology is God, and nothing else but God, revealed in Incarnation, Trinity and Eucharist

Who may marry?

These pictures of marriage are hugely important. The churches need to educate their clergy and leaders about the deep theological structure of marriage in Christian faith so that couples contemplating marriage can see their own marriage as the good news of who God is and what God does. This task is important in its own right. Having examined some of the rich theology of marriage, we can now return to the question posed in the last chapter: whether same-sex couples can marry.

The Church has always regulated who may marry. Based on Leviticus 18.6–18 and 20.17–21, there are 'prohibited degrees' of marriage to close relatives. Spouses must have reached a minimum age. They must be single, and capable of understanding the meaning of consent. The

Roman Catholic Church, following Tradition, prohibits marriage to anyone previously married.[12] There has never been a regulation that marriage should be restricted to a man and a woman. That is because it is assumed. It was an unspoken assumption underlying all the others. The expectation of some lesbian and gay Christian couples that Christian marriage be extended to them therefore opens up a radically new question. It is unprecedented, and if the Church is to open out marriage to couples of the same sex, it would probably be the biggest change to marriage that marriage has ever undergone. The arguments for change are unstoppable, and need to be located first among other historical changes that have happened to marriage.

> There has never been a regulation that marriage should be restricted to a man and a woman

The changing shape of marriage

Since the New Testament there have been many changes. Boys and girls could be betrothed as early as seven, and married as young as 12 and 14.[13] Since God had made women to produce sons, the sooner they tackled their allotted task, the better. King Henry II was married at three and a half.[14] In 2008 in England and Wales the mean age of marriage for single men was 32.1, and for single women, 29.9 years.[15] Until at least the beginning of the second millennium brides were *traded*, and marriages arranged, between families (as they still are in some faiths and societies). Marriage became a sacrament, but only in the twelfth century. Marriage was seen as a process, beginning with betrothal and with the 'spousals'. Only in 1753 does English law make marriage into a single event called a 'wedding'. Protestant churches instigated divorce and remarriage (dubiously claiming scriptural support) and thereby changed one of its meanings for ever.

The purposes of marriage are regularly redefined by the churches. I have compared the marriage services of the Book of Common Prayer (1662) and of *Common Worship* (2000) elsewhere, drawing attention to huge differences in tone and content (as well as some similarities).[16] The greatest change to marriage has been brought about through the European Enlightenment, as women began to be seen first as a separate sex, and then as a sex equal to the male sex. Only in the second half of the twentieth century do women, mainly in the global North, begin to rise to full equality with men with regard to educational and employment opportunities, and so to careers and a place in public spaces occupied only by men. Inside marriage, patriarchy has been largely replaced by partnership, and hierarchy by equality. These gains are very positive, part of the 'world we have won'.[17] Patriarchy 'was the loser of the twentieth century. Probably no other social institution has been forced to retreat as much'.[18] The pictures of marriage painted in this chapter enable the Church to endorse these changes and to praise God for them. The big question remains whether marriage can accommodate same-sex couples.

Picturing same-sex marriage

All seven pictures are applicable to such marriages. Let us imagine a Christian lesbian or gay couple who are devoted to each other, who wish to make the same vows to one another, before God, that straight couples are required to make. They vow to love and cherish each other, 'for better, for worse, for richer, for poorer, in sickness and in health, to love and to cherish, till death us do part'. They will love each other as Christ loves the Church. Their relationship is *a communion of persons* with the hope of growing in deepening love and fruitfulness. Their relationship is *a gift of bodies*, no less a mimesis of Christ's self-giving for us than any straight marriage. Their relationship is *a covenant*: they wish it to be given further covenantal form by asking for marriage and making their vows before God and the congregation. It is as capable of being *an image of the New Covenant* as any straight marriage. They will *minister their sacrament to each other* and discover the grace of God within it. They can become *a unity of heart, body and mind*. Their joy in each other stands as much *an anticipation of the end times*, when all barriers to the triumph of love are broken down, as a straight marriage. These pictures of marriage are truly inclusive.

Objections dismissed

Let us return to the objections raised against the admission of lesbian and gay couples to marriage in Chapter 5. The strongest objections were the definitional, biblical, heterosexual, procreative and natural law ones.

Making sense of marriage

The *definitional objection* assumes that definitions remain constant throughout time, and they do not. This objection tries to settle the question by refusing to allow it to be discussed at all. Marriage just *is* a permanent relationship between a man and a woman.

Marriage has been differently defined by different churches in different periods, and these definitions give rise to similarities and differences. The recognition that married people may divorce and remarry has already changed marriage forever. Our modern understanding of what a man or a woman is differs profoundly from the ancient one. We no longer believe in a single sex, 'man', in which women are inferior and imperfect versions of the more God-like male. We find it convenient (indeed far too easy) to think of two sexes. Without this assumption even the discussion of the possibility of 'same-sex' marriage makes no sense. The issue is rather whether two persons of the same sex are capable of committing themselves to each other in accordance with the seven pictures of marriage described earlier. Clearly they can. Definitions cannot determine the question.

The *biblical objection* has already been refuted. But the objectors appear to be in too much difficulty to be able to admit that the biblical world is markedly different from our own, and one of the differences is the way we think about our bodies. We don't believe that our bodies have four humours (which must be in balance if we are to be healthy); or that women emit sperm; or that evil spirits cause medical conditions. We don't think men having sex with men is a case of overwhelming and misdirected desire that should have its exclusive focus on women. Since we don't think that women are inferior versions of men, we are not horrified by the 'disease of effemination' (Chapter 4), nor are we afraid of catching it. Since the 1870s terms like 'homosexuality' and 'orientation' have entered our language, and on balance their use is helpful. One scientific view of orientation holds that it is 'partly determined genetically at conception, and partly by hormonal influences on the developing foetus in the womb, and that sexual orientation is complete and fixed by the time of birth'.[19] If this explanation is correct, it remains physiological only, so there is much more to add.

Bisexuality is probably more common than previously thought. The *National Health Statistics Report* in the USA reported that 11.4 per cent of women and 4.9 per cent of men aged between 25 and 44 had had at least one same-sex sexual partner in the previous year.[20] This finding will add weight to the conviction that the sexual labels of modernity are imprecise at best, and increasingly less fit for purpose. All Christians, both liberal and conservative, may soon have to stop using these labels. Explanations of sexual preferences are likely to become more complex and less deterministic. Liberal Christians acknowledge that a small minority of people are drawn to people of their own or to either sex, and however hard they scratch their heads they can't think why God should not have made them that way. They think that the 'principle of charity' requires their testimony to be believed, and they want to know why, if first-century views of the person are to be insisted on, opponents of same-sex love seem otherwise content with twenty-first-century medical diagnoses when they go to the doctor.

> The sexual labels of modernity are imprecise at best, and increasingly less fit for purpose

Children

The *heterosexual* and *procreative* objections may look stronger, but can be disposed of readily. I have many times argued that marriage is much more likely to be the best home environment for raising children, so I have no quarrel with conservatives about the connections they make between marriage and children. It all depends on what is meant by 'the proper context for bringing up children'. If the issue here is about whether a gay or lesbian couple can raise adopted or fostered children, the answer is that they clearly can. Given the shortage of homes for children who need them, it is disingenuous to hold that same-sex couples cannot be good adoptive parents either because God has decreed that they should not be parents, or to hold (as conservatives do) that it is better for children not to have an adoptive home than to join one inhabited by a same-sex couple. The American Psychological Association concluded, in its July 2004 'Resolution on Sexual Orientation, Parents, and Children':

Making sense of marriage

> There is no scientific basis for concluding that lesbian mothers or gay fathers are unfit parents on the basis of their sexual orientation... On the contrary, results of research suggest that lesbian and gay parents are as likely as heterosexual parents to provide supportive and healthy environments for their children... Overall, results of research suggest that the development, adjustment, and well-being of children with lesbian and gay parents do not differ markedly from that of children with heterosexual parents.[21]

Churches are right to insist that one of the purposes of marriage is to have children and for the children to share in all the advantages bestowed on them by the marriage vows their parents have made. The procreative objection is soundly as well as intuitively based, but the conservatives do not acknowledge that they offer no objection to heterosexual marriages that are infertile in intent, *prior to the marriage being solemnized*, or to marriages that are thought to be, or known to be, infertile. While statistics are hard to come by, it is likely that many thousands of couples marry in church every year who have no intention of having children, and have based their decision on positive moral and spiritual reasons, such as the pursuit of altruistic careers, or religious vocations. No objection is raised against voluntary childlessness among straight married couples. Why, then, an objection to the fruitlessness of same-sex marriages? The insistence on biological fruitfulness also seems strangely unbiblical. The kingdom of God is often set against the raising of families, consisting of 'children born not of natural descent, nor of human decision or a husband's will, but born of God' (John 1.13). A same-sex couple is able to be 'fertile' and 'fruitful' in a myriad ways other than conceiving children.

> The insistence on biological fruitfulness seems strangely unbiblical

It is strange to see Protestant Christians using the *natural law* objection, since this is almost always found in the Catholic moral tradition. The objective moral order is able to tell them the things that God has unmistakably written on it, and they are unmistakably able to read these things aright. Well, leaving aside the arrogance involved in these claims, there is an obvious counter-claim to be made: same-sex attraction is as much a feature of the objective moral order as its more common counterpart, and is not even confined to the human species. It is 'natural' for everyone who experiences it. It is an elementary mistake to confuse 'some' or 'many' with 'all'. If God has ensured the reproduction of species, it does not follow that every member of every species must engage in reproductive behaviour.

How the sources support same-sex marriage

In Chapter 1 we asked how Christian ethics, and especially sexual ethics, gets done. That took us to the sources. We will now briefly revisit them, to show how the recognition of same-sex unions is fully consistent with them.

Scripture

Couples of the same sex wish to be admitted to marriage under the same terms and conditions as straight men and women. This constitutes an unprecedented, novel situation for churches, and for that reason it is pointless to expect it to be directly addressed in the pages of Scripture. The Bible instead shows us who God is and what God does through Christ and the Spirit. The reign of God, and the new humanity that Christ founds, is characterized by its love of God, neighbours and even enemies.

The rush to find proof-texts proscribing homosexuality has led to arguments based on them at the expense of other biblical passages where same-sex relationships appear without the blink of an eyelid. Narratives about David and Jonathan, Ruth and Naomi, and the centurion and his servant (Matt. 8.5–13; Luke 7.1–10) all suggest that the biblical world is more homosocial and less homophobic than conservative Christians want to believe.[22] There are four references in the Gospel of John to the disciple whom Jesus loved. Theodore Jennings concludes:

> The singling out of one who is loved by Jesus makes clear that some kind of love is at stake other than the love that unites Jesus to the rest of his disciples. The text itself suggests that we should recognize here some form of love that certainly does not contradict the more general love of Jesus for all, but which does set it apart from this general love.

A reasonable conclusion is that this difference points us to a different sphere or dimension of love: love characterized by erotic desire or sexual attraction.[23]

Tradition

Tradition is always changing. Examples of issues where traditional teaching has been reversed or revised include usury, slavery, religious freedom, the moral appraisal of war, and the acceptance of human rights. What causes it to change? Two recent studies show that part of the answer is to be found in a more 'profound understanding of the mystery of Christ', and so in a deeper understanding of Christ's solidarity with people who are made to suffer unjustly and unnecessarily.[24] Homosexuality is another clear example where unjust and unnecessary suffering is directly related to the teachings of churches. That teaching has to change.

Conservative Christians are usually aghast when the tradition of interpretative cruelty is unveiled to them. The darker legacy of the Christian faith is its persecution of Jews, its devaluing of women and people of colour, its employment of slaves, its racism, its harsh treatment of illegitimate children and women accused of being witches, and so on. All of these evils were fanned and encouraged by reading Scripture in just the ways conservative Christians are reading it now with regard to homosexuality.[25] They really must disentangle their zeal for God from their fear of people who are different from them.

> They really must disentangle their zeal for God from their fear of people who are different from them.

Reason in the form of closer, empirical understanding, partial though it may be, also helps to change the understanding of minorities by majorities. We no longer think that black people are black because they are the children of Canaan whom God cursed; that sick people are sick because God is punishing them for their sins; or that poor people are poor because God 'made them high and lowly, and ordered their estate'. In all these cases, greater solidarity with the oppressed, a new understanding of their plight, and a growing sense of the moral and doctrinal inadequacy of earlier teachings, helped to bring about change. Yes, a deeper comprehension of God's love for all people led to an abandonment of these terrible ideas.

Experience, conscience and wisdom

The use of Experience is a most powerful catalyst for change. There are countless examples of death, persecution, violence and discrimination against sexual minorities. Christian theology is contributing directly to these atrocities. Conscience too is a catalyst for change, both the consciences of couples whose lives are open with a clear conscience before God, and the consciences of conservative theologians who, because of their love of God, must one day listen to the unease within themselves that must surely accompany their unhelpful musings about sex. Wisdom, Richard Hooker reminded us, employs all the sources of theological understanding to convince us of God's truth. Our listening to them, and to the victims of an uncharitable and counter-Christian reading of them, forms a unity of conviction. All the sources were given to us in order to love God and our neighbours better. Readers themselves must decide which uses of the sources are more likely to be effective.

7

Making sense of Spirit – from crucifixion to inspiration

There is a little space left in this very short book to ponder how sexual love is able to reunite sexuality and spirituality. Our brief reflection will require a counter-reading of Paul's reflection on 'spirit' and 'flesh' in Galatians 5.13–25.

Crucifying the flesh?

According to a standard reading of Paul, 'flesh' and 'spirit' are at war with one another.[1] That is why Paul exhorts the Galatians:

> So I say, live by the Spirit, and you will not gratify the desires of the flesh. For the flesh desires what is contrary to the Spirit, and the Spirit what is contrary to the flesh. They are in conflict with each other, so that you do not do whatever you want. But if you are led by the Spirit, you are not under law.   (Gal. 5.16–18)

'Those who belong to Christ Jesus', he explains, 'have crucified the flesh with its passions and desires. Since we live by the Spirit, let us keep in step with the Spirit' (Gal. 5.24–25). There is no doubt that this and other similar passages have been recruited to promote an unhealthy dualism, and a suspicion (to say the least) of all sexual activity, even within marriage. However, two important considerations require a rereading and a different estimate of Paul's teaching.

First, the identification of Paul's opponents. These are the Christians who thought that they, and all new converts, were required to keep the Jewish law. They are sometimes called 'Judaizers'. Paul is adamant that Christ has freed them from the constraints of the old law. They must use this freedom responsibly, not misuse it profligately:

> You, my brothers and sisters, were called to be free. But do not use your freedom to indulge the flesh; rather, serve one another in love. The entire law is summed up in a single command: 'Love your neighbour as yourself.' If you keep on biting and devouring each other, watch out or you will be destroyed by each other.
>
> (Gal. 5.13–15)

A good case can be made for claiming that the Judaizers of the *contemporary* Church are those Christians who turn Christian sexual morality into a law. Have sex only when you are married. Don't have sex at all with anyone (even with yourself) if you are single, lesbian, gay, bisexual, divorced, widowed, or a hormone-fuelled randy adolescent. This kind of morality is precisely what the Judaizers wished to import into the churches of Galatia in Paul's absence, and he was very sore about it. It crucifies the soul. Roman Catholics and Evangelicals alike often have to suffer this kind of law-governed approach to sexual morality from their preachers and teachers, even when their laws actually elude diligent readers of the Bible. Many Christians actually 'seek more and more of the pseudo-security that comes from legalism – the outer control of one's life and thought by a strict, detailed code'. They are 'still begging pastors and churches for the false security of other-regulated thought and life'.[2]

Laws and freedoms

A standard, pat answer to the kind of liberal objection I have just made is that it is 'antinomian': that is, that Paul's opponents and liberal-minded Christians ignore the requirement that morality requires laws. They are against (*anti*) laws (*nomoi*). The obvious reply is that Paul does not counter legalism with antinomianism. We have just read how he insists on the responsible use of Christian *freedom*:

> You, my brothers and sisters, were called to be free. But do not use your freedom to indulge the flesh; rather, serve one another in love. The entire law is summed up in a single command: 'Love your neighbour as yourself.'
> (Gal. 5.13–14)

Christians are free in relation to the laws of the First Testament, but are summoned to a greater responsibility, the love of their neighbours in humble service. The practice of this love will in any case lead to the avoidance of promiscuous and exploitative behaviour which laws are supposed to prevent.

> Christians are summoned to a greater responsibility, the love of their neighbours in humble service

Does not the position I have outlined risk or license the very 'indulgence of the flesh' that Paul is plainly warning against? Well, 'flesh and spirit', like 'law and freedom', are antitheses, each 'suggesting the contrast between two different modes or ways of life'.[3] Fortunately, Paul provides illustrations of each. So:

> The acts of the flesh are obvious: sexual immorality, impurity and debauchery; idolatry and witchcraft; hatred, discord, jealousy, fits of rage, selfish ambition, dissensions, factions and envy; drunkenness, orgies, and the like. I warn you, as I did before, that those who live like this will not inherit the kingdom of God. (Gal. 5.19–21)

The 'flesh', then, is illustrated by sexual immorality, debauchery, drunkenness and orgies, among other

> Life in the Spirit is characterized by *love*

fleshly 'acts'. I have never met a Christian who ever advocated these. Life in the Spirit is characterized by *love*.

> But the fruit of the Spirit is love, joy, peace, forbearance, kindness, goodness, faithfulness, gentleness and self-control. Against such things there is no law. Those who belong to Christ Jesus have crucified the flesh with its passions and desires. Since we live by the Spirit, let us keep in step with the Spirit. (Gal. 5.19–25)

The passions and desires of the flesh, insofar as they lead to sexual immorality, debauchery, drunkenness and orgies, are 'crucified'. But life in the Spirit requires passion and desires too.

Life in the Spirit

Paul is concerned with Christian identity, with how groups of Christians should behave. The 'fruit of the Spirit' belongs to interpersonal relations among Christians. It is clear that every one of the nine examples Paul gives is able to be applied to sexual relations. Paul may not have had sex in mind when he wrote about the fruit of the Spirit. He was more worried about the 'acts of the flesh'. But sexual relations belong to interpersonal relations. The claim is, rather, that the way of love is inspired by the Spirit, while the way of selfish indulgence and exploitation can and should be left behind ('crucified'). On this view, a positive, healthy sexuality is able to re-emerge. It remains to show how in the intimacy of shared sexual love, each of the nine fruits can be plucked, shared and enjoyed.

Plucking the fruits

Life in the Spirit elevates the bonding of shared love into a sacrament of mutual self-giving. It releases *love* (*agapè*). Love is a relation where domination is replaced by consideration. Instead of indulging in selfish pleasure, 'rather, serve one another in love. For the entire law is summed up in a single command: "Love your neighbour as yourself."'

Why should the *joy* of life in the Spirit be removed from the intense sexual pleasure God has given us to enjoy? Joy can flood into sexual exchanges as pleasure is given as well as received; as one knows in one's loving that one is loved back, accepted and cherished. It is incumbent on all pastors to commend the joy and pleasure of mutual love, for an abundance of these make divorce and adultery less likely.[4]

Christians exchange the *peace* at the Eucharist. Can there not also be a deep peace after love-making? What better way is there to make up after an inevitable quarrel? Jack Dominian comments, 'There is very little description of the aftermath of intercourse as a soothing, relieving, relaxing experience in which physical and mental discomfort is relieved.'[5]

Is not *forbearance* a vital ingredient in a long-term sexual relationship? Since neither 'I' nor 'my' partner is ever perfect, and we can all often be downright irritating, is not forbearance essential for acceptance of each other's faults, for learning the virtue of patience? The root of Christian faith lies in God's forbearance with us, for (as Paul says), 'God demonstrates his own love for us in this: While we were still sinners, Christ died for us' (Rom. 5.8).

Making sense of Spirit

Is not *kindness* powerfully demonstrated in the countless ways couples administer their sacrament to each other?[6] In the tiny gestures and the larger negotiation of household tasks?

Is not *goodness* also found in countless ways, not least in the contribution that stable couples make to each other, to their children, to their church, and to the overall good of societies? Dominian notes that 'with the passage of time, the initial idealization' with which partners invest each other 'fades'. Yet at that very point, it is possible for 'new depths of goodness and meaning to be found'.[7]

In *faithfulness* couples imitate the very commitment and devotion that God shows in making covenants with God's people.[8]

Gentleness may be learned better in the laboratory of love-making than anywhere else.

And *self-control*, like chastity, is needed, not necessarily for heroic achievements of abstinence, but for the restraint that discourages casual sexual contact in the stony path to sexual maturity, and encourages faithfulness after vows have been solemnly made.

In these pages I have tried to make sense of sex by using Liberal Theology. I think that within the spectrum of available Christian theologies, it sheds more light on sex than alternative standpoints. A mere mortal, I may be wrong. I long for the day when a robust faith in Christ and a joyful sex life are integrated together for all of God's children who seek them, irrespective of their status, sex or orientation.

Notes

1 Making sense of the sources

1 Rowan Williams, 'The Body's Grace', in Eugene F. Rogers, Jr, *Theology and Sexuality: Classic and Contemporary Readings* (Oxford/Malden, MA: Blackwell, 2002), 309–21, p. 310.
2 Callum G. Brown, *The Death of Christian Britain: Understanding Secularization 1800–2000* (London/New York: Routledge, 2009), p. 8.
3 *Catechism of the Catholic Church* (London: Geoffrey Chapman, 1994), para. 365, p. 83, and online at <www.vatican.va/archive/ENG0015/__P1B.HTM>.
4 There is an important distinction to be made between *substantive* and *conceptual* dualism. The first of these assumes people are combinations of two things. The second assumes people are one thing, about which two basic sets of descriptions are required.
5 Adrian Thatcher, *Liberating Sex: A Christian Sexual Theology* (London: SPCK, 1993), pp. 30–40.
6 Harriet Bradley, *Gender* (Cambridge/Malden, MA: Polity Press, 2007), p. 1. Bradley offers several other definitions too.
7 Charles Taylor, *A Secular Age* (Cambridge, MA/London: Belknap Press, 2007), p. 554.
8 Taylor, *A Secular Age*, p. 555. See also pp. 612–17.
9 Donna Freitas, *Sex and the Soul: Judging Sexuality, Spirituality, Romance, and Religion on America's College Campuses* (New York: Oxford University Press, 2008).
10 Freitas, *Sex and the Soul*, p. 219.
11 See John Witte, Jr, *The Sins of the Fathers: The Law and Theology of Illegitimacy Reconsidered* (New York: Cambridge University Press, 2009).
12 Jeffrey Weeks, *The World We Have Won* (London/New York: Routledge, 2007), p. x.
13 For a fuller discussion of the sources for thinking theologically about sex, see Adrian Thatcher, *God, Sex and Gender: An Introduction* (Chichester: Wiley-Blackwell, 2011), pp. 33–54.
14 House of Bishops' Group on Issues in Human Sexuality, *Some Issues in Human Sexuality: A Guide to the Debate* (London: Church House Publishing, 2003), para. 2.1.7, p. 38.

15 Adrian Thatcher, *The Savage Text: The Use and Abuse of the Bible* (Chichester: Wiley-Blackwell, 2008), pp. 25–7.
16 *Catechism*, paras 80–2.
17 The use of the title 'Old Testament' is increasingly problematic in relation to the Hebrew Bible, because for practising Jews now, these scriptures are *living* scriptures, and not 'old' in the sense of 'superseded'. So I have used a different nomenclature in this book – First and Second Testaments. However, I do not pretend this is an ideal solution, or one that is acceptable to all Christians.
18 House of Bishops, *Some Issues*, p. 51, para. 2.4.17.
19 For the arguments, see Thatcher, *God, Sex and Gender*, pp. 38–40.
20 Richard Hooker, *Laws of Ecclesiastical Polity* [1594]. In John Keble (ed.), *The Works of That Learned and Judicious Divine, Mr. Richard Hooker: with an Account of His Life and Death* (Oxford: Clarendon Press, 1876), 2.2.2, p. 290.
21 The New International Version of the Bible is used throughout, unless otherwise indicated.
22 See <www.modchurchunion.org/about/index.htm>.
23 On fundamentalism, see Malise Ruthven, *Fundamentalism: The Search for Meaning* (Oxford: Oxford University Press, 2004).
24 On conservative evangelicalism, see Robert Warner, *Reinventing English Evangelicalism, 1966–2001: A Theological and Sociological Study* (London: Wipf and Stock, 2007).
25 For a full account, see William Countryman, *Dirt, Greed and Sex: Sexual Ethics in the New Testament and their Implications for Today* (London: SCM Press, 1989).
26 For introductions to Liberal Theology see Michael J. Langford, *A Liberal Theology for the Twenty-First Century: A Passion for Reason* (Aldershot: Ashgate, 2001); and Jonathan Clatworthy, *Liberal Faith in a Divided Church* (Ropley: John Hunt Publishing, 2008).
27 See Ian Markham, 'Revisionism', in John Webster, Kathryn Tanner and Iain Torrance (eds), *The Oxford Handbook of Systematic Theology* (Oxford: Oxford University Press, 2007), 600–16, p. 600.

2 Making sense of desire – from repression to expression

1 For the list and a classification, see William Loader, *Sexuality in the New Testament: Understanding the Key Texts* (London: SPCK, 2010), pp. 76–9.
2 Dale Martin, 'Paul without Passion: On Paul's Rejection of Desire in Sex and Marriage', in Dale Martin, *Sex and the Single Savior* (Louisville, KY/London: Westminster John Knox Press, 2006).

3 David Fredrickson, 'Passionless Sex in 1 Thessalonians 4:4–5', *Word and World*, 23, Winter (2003): 23–30.
4 J. Edward Ellis, *Paul and Ancient Views of Sexual Desire* (London: T&T Clark International, 2007), p. 95.
5 Jennifer Wright Knust has written a disturbing monograph on how Christians used sexual slander to discredit their opponents, inside and outside the Church. See her *Abandoned to Lust: Sexual Slander and Ancient Christianity* (New York: Columbia University Press, 2006).
6 Loader, *Sexuality in the New Testament*, pp. 125–6.
7 The sad story of the polemics between them, and the ascetic antics that Jovinian opposed, is told by David Hunter, *Marriage, Celibacy, and Heresy in Ancient Christianity: The Jovinianist Controversy* (Oxford: Oxford University Press, 2007).
8 Peter Brown, *The Body and Society: Men, Women and Sexual Renunciation in Early Christianity* (London: Faber & Faber, 1989), p. 55.
9 See notes 2 and 3 above.
10 Christine Roy Yoder, 'Shaping Desire: A Parent's Attempt: Proverbs 1–9', *Journal for Preachers*, 33.4 (2010): 54–61, p. 54.
11 Karen A. McClintock, *Sexual Shame: An Urgent Call to Healing* (Minneapolis: Fortress Press, 2001), pp. 23–4.
12 McClintock, *Sexual Shame*, p. 24.
13 McClintock, *Sexual Shame*, p. 39.
14 McClintock, *Sexual Shame*, p. 66.
15 Peter Black, 'The Broken Wings of Eros: Christian Ethics and the Denial of Desire', *Theological Studies*, 64.1 (2003): 106–26, p. 107.
16 Black, 'The Broken Wings of Eros', p. 107.
17 Rowan Williams, 'The Body's Grace', in Eugene F. Rogers, Jr, *Theology and Sexuality: Classic and Contemporary Readings* (Oxford/Malden, MA: Blackwell, 2002), 309–21, p. 313.
18 See Adrian Thatcher, *The Savage Text: The Use and Abuse of the Bible* (Chichester: Wiley-Blackwell, 2008), pp. 10–11, and throughout.
19 See Adrian Thatcher, *God, Sex and Gender: An Introduction* (Chichester: Wiley-Blackwell, 2011), pp. 69–72.
20 From the Church of England *Common Worship* Marriage Service, in which Song of Songs 8.6–7 forms part of a permitted reading. Online at <www.churchofengland.org/media/1173941/cw%20pastoral%20services%20marriage%20web.pdf>.
21 Richard Kearney, 'The Shulammite's Song: Divine Eros, Ascending and Descending', in Virginia Burrus and Catherine Keller (eds), *Toward a Theology*

of Eros: Transfiguring Passion at the Limits of Discipline* (New York: Fordham University Press, 2006), 306–40, p. 308.
22. Carey Ellen Walsh, *Exquisite Desire: Religion, the Erotic, and the Song of Songs* (Minneapolis: Augsburg Fortress, 2000), p. 66.
23. Roland Murphy, 'Wisdom and Eros in Proverbs 1–9', *Catholic Biblical Quarterly*, 50 (1988), p. 600.
24. Augustine, *On the Goods of Marriage*, 3. Online at <www.newadvent.org/fathers/1309.htm>.
25. Yoder, 'Shaping Desire', p. 55.
26. See Darlene Weaver, *Self Love and Christian Ethics* (Cambridge: Cambridge University Press, 2002).
27. Julie Hanlon Rubio, *Family Ethics: Practices for Christians* (Washington, DC: Georgetown University Press, 2010), p. 113.
28. Mary D. Pellauer, 'The Moral Significance of Female Orgasm', in James B. Nelson and Sandra P. Longfellow (eds), *Sexuality and the Sacred* (London: Cassell, 1994), p. 156.
29. Williams, 'The Body's Grace', pp. 318–19.

3 Making sense of bodies – from 'sinful bodies' to the Body of Christ

1. Pope Benedict XVI, *Deus Caritas Est* (2005), para. 5. Online at <www.vatican.va/holy_father/benedict_xvi/encyclicals/documents/hf_ben-xvi_enc_20051225_deus-caritas-est_en.html>.
2. There is a huge literature on these concepts and the relation between them, way beyond the scope of this book. For a recent and reliable guide see Werner G. Jeanrond, *A Theology of Love* (London/New York: T&T Clark, 2010).
3. Benedict XVI, *Deus Caritas Est*, para. 5.
4. Benedict XVI, *Deus Caritas Est*, para. 1.
5. Benedict XVI, *Deus Caritas Est*, para. 7.
6. W. Sibley Towner, 'Clones of God: Genesis 1:26–28 and the Image of God in the Hebrew Bible', *Interpretation*, 59.4, October (2005): 341–56, p. 343. These are: 1. A pointer to Christ the image of God. 2. A contrast with the 'likeness' of God. 3. Abstract spiritual endowments such as 'memory, self-awareness, rationality, intelligence, spirituality, even an immortal soul'. 4. Free will. 5. Some human emotions, 'especially love, qualities not shared with animals'. 6. Self-transcendence. 7. The 'external appearance of human beings'. 8. God's deputy on earth. 9. God's partner. 10. The division of humankind into male and female.

7 For a prolonged survey and argument, see Stanley Grenz, *The Social God and the Relational Self: A Trinitarian Theology of the Imago Dei* (Louisville, KY/London: Westminster John Knox Press, 2001).
8 *Gaudium et spes*, para. 24. Online at <www.vatican.va/archive/hist_councils/ii_vatican_council/documents/>.
9 International Theological Commission, *Communion and Stewardship: Human Persons Created in the Image of God* (undated), para. 38. See Chapter 2, 'In the Image of God: Persons in Communion', for the references and the story of its development.
10 Adrian Thatcher, *Marriage after Modernity: Christian Marriage in Postmodern Times* (Sheffield: Sheffield Academic Press/New York: New York University Press, 1999), pp. 225–8; *Theology and Families* (Malden, MA/Oxford: Blackwell, 2007).
11 In particular see John Macmurray, *Persons in Relation* (London: Faber & Faber, 1961).
12 For a fine theological account of this, see Alistair I. McFadyen, *The Call to Personhood: A Christian Theory of the Individual in Social Relationships* (Cambridge: Cambridge University Press, 1990).
13 Todd A. Salzman and Michael G. Lawler, *The Sexual Person: Toward a Renewed Catholic Anthropology* (Washington, DC: Georgetown University Press, 2008), p. 135.
14 Salzman and Lawler, *The Sexual Person*, p. 135.
15 See James D. G. Dunn, *The Theology of Paul the Apostle* (Grand Rapids, MI: Eerdmans, 1998).
16 Anthony Kelly, '"The body of Christ: Amen!": The Expanding Incarnation', *Theological Studies*, 71.4, December (2010): 792–816, pp. 804–5.
17 Diana Swancutt, 'Sexing the Pauline Body of Christ: Scriptural Sex in the Context of the American Christian Culture War', in Virginia Burrus and Catherine Keller (eds), *Toward a Theology of Eros: Transfiguring Passion at the Limits of Discipline* (New York: Fordham University Press, 2006), 65–98, p. 94.
18 See Brian S. Rosner, 'Temple Prostitution in 1 Corinthians 6:12–20', *Novum Testamentum*, 40 (1998).
19 Lorraine Cavanagh, *Making Sense of God's Love: Atonement and Redemption* (London: SPCK, 2011).
20 Adrian Thatcher, *Liberating Sex: A Christian Sexual Theology* (London: SPCK, 1993), p. 41.
21 Timothy Radcliffe OP, 'Paul and Sexual Identity: 1 Corinthians 11:2–16', in Janet Martin Soskice (ed.), *After Eve: Women, Theology and the Christian Tradition* (London: Collins/Marshall Pickering, 1990); *What is the Point*

of Being a Christian? (London/New York: Continuum, 2005); 'This is My Body, Given for You: Christianity and Sexuality', in Timothy Radcliffe and Lytta Basset (eds), *Christians and Sexuality in the Time of Aids* (London/New York: Continuum, 2007).
22 Radcliffe, 'This is My Body', p. 52.
23 Radcliffe, 'This is My Body', p. 53.
24 Radcliffe, 'This is My Body', p. 55.
25 Radcliffe, 'This is My Body', p. 56.
26 Rowan Williams, 'The Body's Grace', in Eugene F. Rogers, Jr, *Theology and Sexuality: Classic and Contemporary Readings* (Oxford/Malden, MA: Blackwell, 2002), 309–21, p. 313.
27 Radcliffe, 'This is My Body', p. 58.
28 Salzman and Lawler, *The Sexual Person*, p. 134 (emphasis added).
29 Salzman and Lawler, *The Sexual Person*, p. 133.
30 Salzman and Lawler, *The Sexual Person*, p. 134.

4 Making sense of sexual difference – from difference to indifference

1 The Lambeth Commission was set up in 2003 by the Archbishop of Canterbury to seek ways of healing the 'impaired communion' which had arisen as a result of divisions over sexuality. Its report (*The Windsor Report*) was produced in 2004.
2 Lambeth Commission on Communion, *The Windsor Report* (2004), para. 87. Online at <www.aco.org/windsor2004/section_b/p10.cfm>.
3 For a full discussion of complementarity, including its various types, see Todd A. Salzman and Michael G. Lawler, *The Sexual Person: Toward a Renewed Catholic Anthropology* (Washington, DC: Georgetown University Press, 2008), pp. 85–91.
4 House of Bishops' Group on Issues in Human Sexuality, *Some Issues in Human Sexuality: A Guide to the Debate* (London: Church House Publishing, 2003), para. 1.2.5, p. 9.
5 House of Bishops, *Some Issues*, para. 1.2.9, p. 10 (emphasis added).
6 House of Bishops, *Some Issues*, p. 327, n.9.
7 Pope John Paul II, *Letter to Women* (1996), para. 7. Online at <www.vatican.va/holy_father/john_paul_ii/letters/documents/hf_jp-ii_let_29061995_women_en.html>.
8 Susannah Cornwall, *Sex and Uncertainty in the Body of Christ* (London: Equinox, 2010).
9 For example, Gilbert Herdt, *Same Sex, Different Cultures* (Colorado Springs: Westview, 1997). And see Christine Gudorf, 'The Erosion of

Sexual Dimorphism', *Journal of the American Academy of Religion*, 69.4, December (2001): 863–91, pp. 874–7.
10. Margaret Farley, *Just Love: A Framework for Christian Sexual Ethics* (London: Continuum, 2006), pp. 152–3.
11. Joseph Galgalo and Debbie Royals, 'Christian Spirituality and Sexuality', in Philip Groves (ed.), *The Anglican Communion and Homosexuality* (London: SPCK, 2008), 239–65, p. 245.
12. Winston Halapua, '*Moana* Waves: Oceania and Homosexuality', in Terry Brown (ed.), *Other Voices, Other Worlds: The Global Church Speaks out on Homosexuality* (London: Darton, Longman and Todd, 2006), pp. 26–39.
13. Halapua, '*Moana* Waves', p. 26.
14. For much of the detail that follows see Thomas Laqueur, *Making Sex: Body and Gender from the Greeks to Freud* (Cambridge, MA/London: Harvard University Press, 1990).
15. See William Loader, *Sexuality in the New Testament: Understanding the Key Texts* (London: SPCK, 2010), p. 43.
16. Emphasis added. The King James Version is the most literal and faithful translation of this verse. Moreover, it accords better with what English translators in 1611 would have thought about women making sperm.
17. Mathew Kuefler, *The Manly Eunuch: Masculinity, Gender Ambiguity, and Christian Ideology in Late Antiquity* (Chicago/London: University of Chicago Press, 2001), p. 22.
18. Diana Swancutt, '"The Disease of Effemination": The Charge of Effeminacy and the Verdict of God (Romans 1:18–26)', in Stephen D. Moore and Janice Capel Anderson (eds), *New Testament Masculinities* (Atlanta, GA: Society of Biblical Literature, 2003), 193–234, p. 198.
19. Pope John Paul II, 'Authentic Concept of Conjugal Love', *Origins*, 28, 4 March (1999), p. 655. Cited in Salzman and Lawler, *The Sexual Person*, p. 87.
20. Salzman and Lawler, *The Sexual Person*, p. 87.
21. Jane Shaw, 'Reformed and Enlightened Church', in Gerard Loughlin (ed.), *Queer Theology: Rethinking the Western Body* (Malden, MA/Oxford: Blackwell, 2007), 215–29, p. 227.
22. For some of these see Harriet Bradley, *Gender* (Cambridge/Malden, MA: Polity Press, 2007), pp. 1–25.
23. Bradley, *Gender*, p. 1.
24. Bradley, *Gender*, p. 6.
25. Adrian Thatcher, *God, Sex and Gender: An Introduction* (Chichester: Wiley-Blackwell, 2011), p. 20.
26. Gudorf, 'The Erosion of Sexual Dimorphism', p. 880.
27. Gudorf, 'The Erosion of Sexual Dimorphism', p. 881.

28 See Mary McClintock Fulkerson and Sheila Briggs, 'Introduction', in Mary McClintock Fulkerson and Sheila Briggs (eds), *The Oxford Handbook of Feminist Theology* (Oxford: Oxford University Press, 2012), 1–20, and several other essays in the volume.
29 Graham Ward, 'There is No Sexual Difference', in Loughlin (ed.), *Queer Theology*, 76–85, p. 76.
30 Colleen M. Conway, *Behold the Man: Jesus and Greco-Roman Masculinity* (Oxford: Oxford University Press, 2008), p. 99 (emphasis added).
31 Miroslav Volf, 'The Trinity and Gender Identity', in D. A. Campbell (ed.), *Gospel and Gender: A Trinitarian Engagement with being Male and Female in Christ* (London/New York: T&T Clark International, 2003), 155–78, p. 170 (emphasis in original).
32 Volf, 'The Trinity and Gender Identity', p. 173.
33 Cornwall, *Sex and Uncertainty*, p. 73.
34 Cornwall, *Sex and Uncertainty*, p. 74.

5 Making sense of homosexuality – from disgust to delight

1 Adrian Thatcher, *The Savage Text: The Use and Abuse of the Bible* (Chichester: Wiley-Blackwell, 2008), Chapters 1 and 2; *God, Sex and Gender: An Introduction* (Chichester: Wiley-Blackwell, 2011), Chapters 9 and 10.
2 *Anglican Theological Review*, 93.1, Winter (2011).
3 John E. Goldingay, Grant R. LeMarquand, George R. Sumner and Daniel A. Westberg, 'Same-Sex Marriage and Anglican Theology: A View from the Traditionalists', *Anglican Theological Review*, 93.1, Winter (2011): 1–50, p. 1.
4 Goldingay, 'Same-Sex Marriage', pp. 24, 26, 30.
5 Goldingay, 'Same-Sex Marriage', p. 9. See also pp. 12, 26.
6 Goldingay, 'Same-Sex Marriage', p. 11.
7 Goldingay, 'Same-Sex Marriage', p. 21. See also pp. 43–4.
8 Goldingay, 'Same-Sex Marriage', p. 16.
9 Goldingay, 'Same-Sex Marriage', p. 26.
10 Goldingay, 'Same-Sex Marriage', p. 28.
11 Goldingay, 'Same-Sex Marriage', p. 30.
12 Goldingay, 'Same-Sex Marriage', pp. 36–42.
13 Goldingay, 'Same-Sex Marriage', p. 31 (emphasis in original). See pp. 31–6.
14 Goldingay, 'Same-Sex Marriage', p. 47.
15 Goldingay, 'Same-Sex Marriage', p. 46.
16 Deirdre J. Good, Willis J. Jenkins, Cynthia B. Kitteredge and Eugene F. Rogers, Jr, 'A Theology of Marriage including Same-Sex Couples: A View

from the Liberals', *Anglican Theological Review*, 93.1, Winter (2011): 51–88, p. 51 (emphasis added).

17 Good, 'A Theology of Marriage', p. 62.
18 Good, 'A Theology of Marriage', p. 62.
19 This argument was strongly emphasized by The Episcopal Church when invited to defend its appointment of a gay, partnered man to the episcopacy. See Office of Communication, The Episcopal Church Center, *To Set our Hope on Christ* (New York: 2005), pp. 8–17.
20 Good, 'A Theology of Marriage', p. 54.
21 Good, 'A Theology of Marriage', p. 69.
22 Good, 'A Theology of Marriage', p. 53.
23 Deirdre J. Good, Willis J. Jenkins, Cynthia B. Kitteredge and Eugene F. Rogers, Jr, 'The Liberal Response', *Anglican Theological Review*, 93.1, Winter (2011): 101–11, p. 104.
24 For the robust rejection, see John E. Goldingay, Grant R. LeMarquand, George R. Sumner and Daniel A. Westberg, 'The Traditionalist Response', *Anglican Theological Review*, 93.1, Winter (2011): 89–100.
25 Mark D. Jordan, 'A Response from Mark D. Jordan', *Anglican Theological Review*, 93.1, Winter (2011), 123–5, p. 125.
26 Deborah Cameron and Don Kulick, *Language and Sexuality* (Cambridge: Cambridge University Press, 2003), p. 21.
27 See, for example, Gareth Moore OP, *A Question of Truth: Christianity and Homosexuality* (London/New York: Continuum, 2003), p. 71.
28 James Alison, *Undergoing God: Dispatches from the Scene of a Break-In* (London/New York: Continuum, 2006), pp. 124–5.
29 Goldingay, 'Same-Sex Marriage', p. 27.
30 See, for example, Dale Martin, *Sex and the Single Savior* (Louisville, KY/ London: Westminster John Knox Press, 2006), pp. 37–50.
31 Jordan, 'A Response', p. 124.
32 See <www.courage.org.uk/>.
33 Jeremy Marks, *Exchanging the Truth of God for a Lie* (Horsham: Roper Penberthy, 2008), p. viii.
34 Good, 'The Liberal Response', p. 106.
35 Good, 'The Liberal Response', p. 105.
36 See Thatcher, *The Savage Text*.
37 Diana Swancutt, '"The Disease of Effemination:" The Charge of Effeminacy and the Verdict of God (Romans 1:18–26)', in Stephen D. Moore and Janice Capel Anderson (eds), *New Testament Masculinities* (Atlanta, GA: Society of Biblical Literature, 2003), 193–234, p. 197.
38 See Saul Olyan, '"And with a male you shall not lie the lying down of a

woman": On the Meaning and Significance of Leviticus 18:22 and 20:13', *Journal of the History of Sexuality*, 5 (1994), pp. 179–206; and Daniel Boyarin, 'Against Rabbinic Sexuality: Textual Reasoning and the Jewish Theology of Sex', in G. Loughlin (ed.), *Queer Theology: Rethinking the Western Body* (Malden, MA/Oxford: Blackwell, 2007), pp. 131–46.

39 Colleen M. Conway, *Behold the Man: Jesus and Greco-Roman Masculinity* (Oxford: Oxford University Press, 2008), p. 50.

40 Diana Swancutt, '"The Disease of Effemination"; and 'Sexing the Pauline Body of Christ: Scriptural Sex in the Context of the American Christian Culture War', in Virginia Burrus and Catherine Keller (eds), *Toward a Theology of Eros: Transfiguring Passion at the Limits of Discipline* (New York: Fordham University Press, 2006), p. 76.

41 Conway, *Behold the Man*, p. 19.

42 M. W. Gleason, *Making Men: Sophists and Self-Presentation in Ancient Rome* (Princeton, NJ: Princeton University Press, 1995), p. xxii.

43 See Thatcher, *God, Sex and Gender*, pp. 163–8 for the range of discussion.

44 S. K. Stowers, *A Rereading of Romans* (New Haven, CT: Yale University Press, 1994), pp. 45–6.

45 Derrick Sherwin Bailey, *Homosexuality and the Western Christian Tradition* (London: Longmans, Green & Co., 1955).

46 H. Kimball-Jones, *Towards a Christian Understanding of the Homosexual* (London: SCM Press, 1967).

47 Norman Pittenger, *Time for Consent* (London: SCM Press, 1970).

6 Making sense of marriage – from patriarchy to partnership

1 For a sensible discussion, see David Blankenhorn, Don Browning and Mary Stewart Van Leeuwen (eds), *Does Christianity Teach Male Headship?* (Grand Rapids, MI/Cambridge: Eerdmans, 2004).

2 See, for example, Stephanie Coontz, *Marriage, a History: From Obedience to Intimacy or How Love Conquered Marriage* (New York: Viking Penguin, 2005).

3 David Matzko McCarthy, 'The Relationship of Bodies: A Nuptial Hermeneutics of Same-sex Unions', in Eugene F. Rogers, Jr (ed.), *Theology and Sexuality: Classic and Contemporary Readings* (Oxford/Malden, MA: Blackwell, 2002), p. 201.

4 *Gaudium et spes*, para. 48. Online at <www.vatican.va/archive/hist_councils/ii_vatican_council/documents/>.

5 For the full story see John Witte, Jr, *From Sacrament to Contract: Marriage, Religion, and Law in the Western Tradition* (Louisville, KY: Westminster John Knox Press, 1997), pp. 74–129.

6 For an extensive discussion of 'covenant' in relation to marriage, see Adrian Thatcher, *Marriage after Modernity: Christian Marriage in Postmodern Times* (Sheffield: Sheffield Academic Press/New York: New York University Press, 1999), pp. 68–77, 87–95.
7 From the list in Paul F. Palmer SJ, 'Christian Marriage: Contract or Covenant?', *Theological Studies*, 33 (1972): 617–65, p. 639.
8 John Paul II, *Familiaris consortio* (1981), section 12, 'Marriage and Communion between God and People'. Online at <www.vatican.va/holy_father/john_paul_ii/apost_exhortations/documents/hf_jp-ii_exh_19811122_familiaris-consortio_en.html>.
9 *Common Worship* Marriage Service. Online at <www.churchofengland.org/prayer-worship/worship/texts/pastoral/marriage/marriage.aspx> (emphasis added).
10 'The Form of Solemnization of Matrimony', Book of Common Prayer (1662). Online at <www.eskimo.com/~lhowell/bcp1662/occasion/marriage.html>.
11 For an exhaustive treatment of the subject, see Adrian Thatcher, *Living Together and Christian Ethics* (Cambridge: Cambridge University Press, 2002).
12 How far this teaching is 'traditional', and for exceptions, see the brief but incisive account of Michael G. Lawler, *What Is and What Ought to Be* (New York/London: Continuum, 2005), pp. 144–53.
13 Christopher Brooke, *The Medieval Idea of Marriage* (Oxford: Clarendon Press, 1989), p. 137.
14 Brooke, *The Medieval Idea of Marriage*, p. 140, n. 51.
15 Online at <www.statistics.gov.uk/STATBASE/Product.asp?vlnk=14275>. The median ages were 30.8 and 28.8 years respectively.
16 Adrian Thatcher, *God, Sex and Gender: An Introduction* (Chichester: Wiley-Blackwell, 2011), pp. 82–5.
17 See Chapter 1, pp. 6–7.
18 Göran Therborn, *Between Sex and Power: Family in the World, 1900–2000* (London/New York: Routledge, 2005), p. 73. However, Therborn also documents the frightening amount of progress that has yet to be made.
19 Gillian Cooke and Alan Sheard, *Homosexuality in the 21st Century* (MCU Forewords Publication, 2009), p. 2.
20 See Andrew Goddard and Glynn Harrison, *Church Times*, 7760, 9 December (2011), p. 13.
21 William Meezan and Jonathan Rauch, 'Gay Marriage, Same-Sex Parenting, and America's Children', *The Future of Children*, 15.2, Fall (2005): 97–115, p. 102. And see pp. 103–4 for the authors' agreement with the conclusions of the American Psychological Association.

22 For the latest treatment of these stories, see Keith Sharpe, *The Gay Gospels: Good News for Lesbian, Gay, Bisexual, and Transgendered People* (Winchester/Washington, DC: O-Books, 2011).
23 Theodore W. Jennings, Jr, *The Man Jesus Loved: Homoerotic Narratives from the New Testament* (Cleveland, OH: Pilgrim Press, 2003), p. 22.
24 Marciano Vidal, 'Progress in the Moral Tradition', in Charles E. Curran (ed.), *Change in Official Catholic Moral Teachings: Readings in Moral Theology, No. 13* (New York/Mahwah, NJ: Paulist Press, 2003), p. 323. And see John T. Noonan, Jr, 'Development in Moral Doctrine', in the same volume.
25 For the full story, and for the arguments, see Adrian Thatcher, *The Savage Text: The Use and Abuse of the Bible* (Chichester: Wiley-Blackwell, 2008).

7 Making sense of Spirit – from crucifixion to inspiration

1 See above, pp. 17–18.
2 Henry H. Mitchell, 'Galatians 5:22–23', *Review & Expositor*, 91.2, Spring (1994): 239–44, p. 239.
3 Bernard O. Ukwuegbu, 'Paraenesis, Identity-defining Norms, or Both? Galatians 5:13–6:10 in the Light of Social Identity Theory', *Catholic Biblical Quarterly*, 70.3, July (2008): 538–59, p. 539.
4 Julie Hanlon Rubio, *Family Ethics: Practices for Christians* (Washington, DC: Georgetown University Press, 2010), pp. 102–6.
5 Jack Dominian, *Let's Make Love: The Meaning of Sexual Intercourse* (London: Darton, Longman and Todd, 2001), p. 69.
6 See above, p. 73.
7 Dominian, *Let's Make Love*, p. 67.
8 See above, pp. 71–3.

Further reading

Bradley, Harriet, *Gender* (Cambridge/Malden, MA: Polity Press, 2007).
Brooten, Bernadette, *Love Between Women: Early Christian Responses to Female Homoeroticism* (Chicago/London: University of Chicago Press, 1998).
Brown, Peter, *The Body and Society: Men, Women and Sexual Renunciation in Early Christianity* (London: Faber & Faber, 1989).
Conway, Colleen M., *Behold the Man: Jesus and Greco-Roman Masculinity* (Oxford: Oxford University Press, 2008).
Coontz, Stephanie, *Marriage, a History: From Obedience to Intimacy or How Love Conquered Marriage* (New York: Viking Penguin, 2005).
Cornwall, Susannah, *Sex and Uncertainty in the Body of Christ* (London: Equinox, 2010).
Countryman, William, *Dirt, Greed and Sex: Sexual Ethics in the New Testament and their Implications for Today* (London: SCM Press, 1989).
Dominian, Jack, *Let's Make Love: The Meaning of Sexual Intercourse* (London: Darton, Longman and Todd, 2001).
Ellison, Marvin M. and Kelly Brown Douglas (eds) *Sexuality and the Sacred, Second Edition: Sources for Theological Reflection* (Louisville, KY: Westminster John Knox Press, 2010).
Farley, Margaret, *Just Love: A Framework for Christian Sexual Ethics* (London: Continuum, 2006).
Jennings, Theodore, W., Jr, *Jacob's Wound: Homoerotic Narrative in the Literature of Ancient Israel* (New York/London: Continuum, 2005).
Jennings, Theodore, W., Jr, *The Man Jesus Loved: Homoerotic Narratives from the New Testament* (Cleveland, OH: Pilgrim Press, 2003).
Jordan, Mark D., *The Ethics of Sex* (Oxford/Malden, MA: Blackwell, 2002).
Jordan, Mark D., *The Silence of Sodom: Homosexuality in Modern Catholicism* (Chicago/London: University of Chicago Press, 2000).
Knust, Jennifer Wright, *Unprotected Texts: The Bible's Surprising Contradictions about Sex and Desire* (New York: HarperOne, 2011).
Kuefler, Mathew, *The Manly Eunuch: Masculinity, Gender Ambiguity, and Christian Ideology in Late Antiquity* (Chicago/London: University of Chicago Press, 2001).
Linzey, Andrew and Richard Kirker (eds), *Gays and the Future of Anglicanism: Responses to the Windsor Report* (Ropley: O-Books, 2005).
Loader, William, *Sexuality in the New Testament: Understanding the Key Texts* (London: SPCK, 2010).

Further reading

Moore, Gareth, OP, *A Question of Truth: Christianity and Homosexuality* (London/New York: Continuum, 2003).

Rogers, Eugene F., Jr (ed.), *Theology and Sexuality: Classic and Contemporary Readings* (Oxford/Malden, MA: Blackwell, 2002).

Salzman, Todd A. and Michael G. Lawler, *The Sexual Person: Toward a Renewed Catholic Anthropology* (Washington, DC: Georgetown University Press, 2008).

Sharpe, Keith, *The Gay Gospels: Good News for Lesbian, Gay, Bisexual, and Transgendered People* (Winchester/Washington, DC: O-Books, 2011).

Thatcher, Adrian, *God, Sex and Gender: An Introduction* (Chichester: Wiley-Blackwell, 2011).

Thatcher, Adrian, *The Savage Text: The Use and Abuse of the Bible* (Chichester: Wiley-Blackwell, 2008).

Weeks, Jeffrey, *The World We Have Won* (London/New York: Routledge, 2007).

Wiesner-Hanks, Merry, *Christianity and Sexuality in the Early Modern World: Regulating Desire, Reforming Practice* (London/New York: Routledge, 2000).

Williams, Rowan, 'The Body's Grace', in Eugene F. Rogers, Jr (ed.), *Theology and Sexuality: Classic and Contemporary Readings* (Oxford/Malden, MA: Blackwell, 2002).

Witte, John, Jr, *From Sacrament to Contract: Marriage, Religion, and Law in the Western Tradition* (Louisville, KY: Westminster John Knox Press, 1997).